T0208510

The War of Gods

Critical Studies in Latin American and Iberian Cultures

James Dunkerley
John King

This major series – the first of its kind to appear in English – is designed to map the field of contemporary Latin American culture, which has enjoyed increasing popularity in Britain and the United States in recent years.

The series aims to broaden the scope of criticism of Latin American culture, which tends still to extol the virtues of a few established 'master' works and to examine cultural production within the context of twentieth-century history. These clear, accessible studies are aimed at those who wish to know more about some of the most important and influential cultural works and movements of our time.

The War of Gods

Religion and Politics in Latin America

Michael Löwy

VERSO

London • New York

First published by Verso 1996
© Michael Löwy
All rights reserved

www.versobooks.com

Verso is the imprint of New Left Books

ISBN: 978-1-85984-002-3

British Library Cataloguing in Publication Data
A catalogue record for this book is available from the British Library

Library of Congress Cataloging-in-Publication Data
Löwy, Michael, 1938–
The war of gods : religion and politics in Latin America /
Michael Löwy.
p.   cm.
Includes bibliographical references and index.
ISBN: 978-1-85984-002-3
1. Liberation theology. 2. Church and state—Latin America.
3. Church and social problems—Latin America. 4. Religion
and politics—Latin America. I. Title.
BT83.57.L69   1996
261.7′098—dc20   96–12017
CIP

Typeset by Keystroke, Jacaranda Lodge, Wolverhampton
Printed and bound in Great Britain by Biddles Ltd,
Guildford and King's Lynn

Contents

Introduction

There exists already a significant body of literature on the relationship between religion and politics in Latin America. Not only theological essays, testimonies of participants and journalistic inquiries, but also academic works belonging to various disciplines of the social sciences (sociology, political science, anthropology) deal – explicitly or not – with this issue. However, most of this research is limited to case studies of a single country (or of a sub-region like Central America), or of a single aspect (the base communities, the new Protestant Churches, etc) of this vast problematic area.

This book is an attempt to provide a general analytical introduction to the study of the new developments in the political/religious field of force during the last thirty-five years in Latin America, in so far as they have been important factors in social change. This chronology is not arbitrary: in the late 1950s a new period in the history of the relations between religion and politics began in Latin America, which is still ongoing and open-ended. Its origins can be found in two historical events that took place almost simultaneously in 1958–59: one in the Vatican – the election of Pope John XXIII – and the other in a Caribbean island: the victory of the Cuban Revolution.

Of course, this book draws heavily upon the available literature, but it tries at the same time to propose a broader picture and to formulate some new theoretical hypotheses. The method it uses is that of a *sociology of culture*, largely inspired by the Marxist tradition (but also incorporating some key Weberian notions). It will therefore focus not on the ethnological description of religious practices, on the study of the functional structure of the Church as an institution, or on the empirical data about the

1

electoral behaviour of various confessions, but, rather, on the complex evolution of the links between religious and political *cultures*, in a context of modernization and intense social and political conflict. Religious documents (theological, canonical or pastoral) will be one of the important source-materials, examined at the same time for their inner cultural content, their social and political implications, and their links to institutions and social movements.

Greater attention will be paid to the religious movements committed to social emancipatory aims – usually called 'progressive' or 'leftist', but these terms are not very adequate – both because of the personal sympathies of the author, and because they constitute a new sociological and historical phenomenon, compared to the traditional conservative role of religion, or to older organizations such as Christian Democracy, already studied in the past. This phenomenon, often designated 'liberation theology', is much deeper and broader than a theological current: as a matter of fact, it is a vast *social movement* – which I propose to designate 'liberationist Christianity' – with far-reaching political consequences. The book will also take into acount the conservative (both Catholic and Protestant) counter-offensive, and its struggle against liberation theology, which has created growing difficulties for this movement. There is no attempt to be exhaustive, and the general hypothesis will be tested against a few case studies.

The expression 'war of gods' is a reference to Weber's well-known argument about the polytheism of values and the unbridgeable conflict of ultimate beliefs ('gods') in modern society. For instance, in *Science as Vocation* (1919) Weber wrote: 'So long as life remains immanent and is interpreted in its own terms, it knows only of an unceasing struggle of these gods with one another. Or speaking directly, the ultimately possible attitudes toward life are irreconcilable, and hence their struggle can never be brought to a final conclusion. Thus it is necessary to make a decisive choice.'[1]

Weber's *Kampf der Götter* very adequately defines the political/ religious ethos of Latin America during the past thirty-five years. On one hand, *ad intra*, it applies to the conflict inside the religious field between radically opposed conceptions of God: those of the progressive and those of the conservative Christians (both Catholic and Protestant) – a 'collision of values' (*Wertkollision* – another

Weberian term) – that can take, in extreme situations such as Central America during the 1980s, even the form of civil war. On the other hand, *ad extra*, the expression has been used by the liberation theologians themselves – without reference to Weber – to describe the conflict between the liberating God, as they conceive him, and the idols of oppression represented by Money, the Market, Commodity, Capital, etc.[2]

Born and raised in Brazil in a family of Jewish immigrants, politically and intellectually linked to the Marxist tradition, I feel at the same time intimacy (as a Latin American) with and distance (as a non-believer) from the object of study. I have no intention of denying my ethical and political sympathy for those Christians who have cast their lot with the struggle for the self-emancipation of the poor in Latin America; but I hope this book may be read with profit also by those who do not share my values and choices.

1

Religion and Politics: Revisiting Marx and Weber

Marxism and Religion: Opium of the People?

Is religion still, as Marx and Engels saw it in the nineteenth century, a bulwark of reaction, obscurantism and conservatism? Is it a sort of narcotic, intoxicating the masses and preventing them from clear-sighted thought and action in their own interests? To a large extent, the answer is *yes*. Their view applies very well to the fundamentalist currents of the main confessions (Christian, Jewish or Muslim), to Catholic conservatism, to most evangelical groups (and their expression in the so-called 'Electronic Church'), and to the majority of the new religious sects – some of which, like the notorious Moon Church, are nothing but a skilful combination of financial manipulation, obscurantist brainwashing and fanatical anti-communism.

However, the emergence of revolutionary Christianity and liberation theology in Latin America (and elsewhere) opens a new historical chapter and raises exciting new questions which cannot be answered without a renewal of the Marxist analysis of religion. Initially, when confronted with such phenomena, Marxists would apply a traditional model of interpretation which counterposed Christian workers and peasants, who could be considered as supporters of the revolution, to the Church (the clergy), a thoroughly reactionary body. As late as 1966, they could still view the death of a priest, Father Camilo Torres, who had joined the Colombian guerrillas and was killed in a confrontation with the army that year, as an exceptional case. But the growing commitment of Christians – including many religious and priests – to popular struggles, and their massive involvement in the Sandinista Revolution, clearly showed the need for a new approach. Marxists who are disconcerted or confused by these developments still resort to the usual distinction between the valid social practice of these Christians, and their religious ideology, defined as necessarily regressive and idealist. However, with liberation theology we see the appearance of religious thinking using Marxist concepts and inspiring struggles for social liberation.

In fact, something new has happened on the Latin American religious scene during the last few decades, the importance of which is world historical. A significant sector of the Church – both believers and clergy – in Latin America has changed its position in the field of social struggle, going over with its material and spiritual resources to the side of the poor and their fight for a new society. Can Marxism help us to explain this unexpected event?

The well-known phrase 'religion is the opium of the people' is considered as the quintessence of the Marxist conception of the religious phenomenon by most of its supporters *and* its opponents. How far is this an accurate viewpoint? First of all, one should emphasize that this statement is *not at all specifically Marxist*. The same phrase can be found, in various contexts, in the writings of Kant, Herder, Feuerbach, Bruno Bauer, Moses Hess and Heinrich Heine. For instance, in his essay on Ludwig Börne (1840), Heine already uses it, in a rather positive (although ironical) way: 'Welcome be a religion that pours into the bitter chalice of the suffering human species some sweet, soporific drops of spiritual opium, some drops of love, hope and faith.' Moses Hess, in his essays published in Switzerland in 1843, takes a more critical (but still ambiguous) stance: 'Religion can make bearable . . . the unhappy consciousness of serfdom . . . in the same way as opium is of good help in painful diseases.'[1]

The expression appeared shortly afterwards in Marx's article on Hegel's *Philosophy of Right* (1844). An attentive reading of the Marxian paragraph where this phrase appears reveals that it is more qualified and less one-sided than is usually believed. Although he is obviously critical of religion, Marx takes into account the *dual character* of the phenomenon: 'Religious distress is at the same time the *expression* of real distress and the *protest* against real distress. Religion is the sigh of the oppressed creature, the heart of a heartless world, just as it is the spirit of an un-spiritual situation. It is the *opiate* of the people.'[2]

If one reads the whole essay, it becomes clear that Marx's viewpoint owed more to left neo-Hegelianism, which saw religion as the alienation of the human essence, than to Enlightenment philosophy, which simply denounced it as a clerical conspiracy. In fact when Marx wrote the above passage he was still a disciple of Feuerbach, and a neo-Hegelian. His analysis of religion was therefore 'pre-Marxist', without any class reference, and rather ahistorical. But it had a *dialectical* quality, grasping the contra-dictory character of the religious 'distress': both a legitimation of existing conditions and a protest against them.

It was only later, particularly in *The German Ideology* (1846), that the proper Marxist study of religion as a *social and historical reality* began. The key element of this new method for the analysis of religion is to approach it as one of the many forms of ideology – that is, of the *spiritual production* of a people, of the production of ideas, representations and consciousness, necessarily conditioned by material production and the corresponding social relations. Although from time to time he uses the concept of 'reflection' – which led several generations of Marxists into a sterile sidetrack – the key idea of the book is the need to explain the genesis and development of the various forms of consciousness (religion, ethics, philosophy, etc) by the social relations, 'by which means, of course, the whole thing can be depicted in its totality (and therefore, too, the reciprocal action of these various sides on one another)'.[3] A whole 'dissident' school of Marxist sociology of culture (Lukács, Goldmann) favours the dialectical concept of *totality* instead of the theory of *reflection*.

After writing, with Engels, *The German Ideology*, Marx paid very little attention to religion as such – that is, as a specific cultural-ideological universe of meaning. One can find, however, in the first volume of *Capital*, some interesting methodological remarks; for instance, the well-known footnote where he answers the argument according to which the importance of politics in Ancient times, and of religion in the Middle Ages, reveals the inadequacy of the materialist interpretation of history: 'Neither could the Middle Age live from Catholicism, nor Antiquity from politics. The respective economic conditions explain, in fact, why Catholicism there and politics here played the dominant role [*Hauptrolle*].'[4] Marx never bothered to provide the economic reasons for the importance of medieval religion, but this passage is significant, because it acknowledges that, under certain historical circumstances, religion can indeed play a decisive role in the life of a society.

In spite of his general lack of interest in religion, Marx paid attention to the relationship between Protestantism and capitalism. Several passages in *Capital* make reference to the contribution of Protestantism to the primitive accumulation of capital – for instance by stimulating the expropriation of Church property and communal pastures. In the *Grundrisse* he makes – half a century before Max Weber's famous essay – the following illuminating comment on the intimate association between Protestantism and capitalism:

> The cult of money has its asceticism, its self-denial, its self-sacrifice – economy and frugality, contempt for mundane, temporal and fleeting pleasures; the chase after the *eternal* treasure. Hence the connection [*Zusammenhang*] between English Puritanism or Dutch Protestantism and money-making [*Geldmachen*].[5]

The parallel (but not identity) with Weber's thesis is astonishing – the more so since the author of *The Protestant Ethic* could not have read this passage (the *Grundrisse* was published for the first time in 1940).

On the other hand, Marx often referred to capitalism as a 'religion of daily life' based on the fetishism of commodity. He described capital as 'a Moloch that requires the whole world as a due sacrifice', and capitalist progress as a 'monstrous pagan god, that only wanted to drink nectar in the skulls of the dead'. His critique of political economy is peppered with references to idolatry: Baal, Moloch, Mammon, the Golden Calf, and, of course, the concept of 'fetish' itself. But this language has rather more a metaphorical than a substantial meaning (in terms of sociology of religion).[6]

Friedrich Engels displayed (probably because of his pietist upbringing) a much greater interest than Marx in religious phenomena and their historic role. Engels's main contribution to the Marxist study of religions is his analysis of the relationship of religious representations to *class struggle*. Over and above the philosophical polemic of 'materialism against idealism', he was interested in understanding and explaining concrete social and historical forms of religion. Christianity no longer appeared (as it had to Feuerbach) as a timeless 'essence', but as a cultural system undergoing transformations in different historical periods: first as a religion of the slaves, later as the state ideology of the Roman Empire, then tailored to feudal hierarchy, and finally adapted to bourgeois society. It thus appears as a symbolic space fought over by antagonistic social forces – in the sixteenth century, for instance, by feudal theology, bourgeois Protestantism and plebeian heresies.

Occasionally his analysis slips towards a narrowly utilitarian, instrumental interpretation of religious movements: ' . . . each of the different classes uses its own appropriate religion . . . and it makes little difference whether these gentlemen believe in their respective religions or not'.[7] Engels seems to find nothing but the 'religious disguise' of class interests in the different forms of belief. However, thanks to his class-struggle method, he realized – unlike the Enlightenment philosophers – that the clergy was not a socially homogeneous body: at certain historical conjunctures, it divided itself according to its class composition. Thus during the Reformation we have on the one side the high clergy, the feudal summit of the hierarchy, and on the other the lower clergy, which supplied the ideologues of the Reformation and of the revolutionary peasant movement.[8]

While he was a materialist, an atheist and an irreconcilable enemy of religion, Engels nevertheless grasped, like the young Marx, the *dual* character of the phenomenon: its role in legitimating the established order but also, according to social circumstances, its critical, protesting and even revolutionary role. Furthermore, most of the concrete studies he wrote concerned the *rebellious* forms of religion.

First of all, he was interested in *primitive Christianity*, which he defined as the religion of the poor, the banished, the damned, the persecuted and the oppressed. The first Christians came from the lowest levels of society: slaves, free men who had been deprived of their rights and small peasants who were crippled by debts.[9] He even went so far as to draw an astonishing parallel between this primitive Christianity and modern socialism: (a) the two great movements are not the creation of leaders and prophets – although prophets are never in short supply in either of them – but are mass movements; (b) both are movements of the oppressed, suffering persecution, their members proscribed and hunted down by the ruling authorities; and (c) both preach an imminent liberation from slavery and misery. To embellish his comparison Engels, somewhat provocatively, quoted a saying of the French historian Renan: 'If you want to get an idea of what the first Christian communities were like, take a look at a local branch of the International Workingmen's Association.'

According to Engels, the parallel between socialism and early Christianity is present in all movements that dream, throughout the centuries, of restoring the primitive Christian religion – from the Taborites of John Zizka ('of glorious memory') and the Anabaptists of Thomas Münzer to (after 1830) the French revolutionary communists and the partisans of the German utopian communist Wilhelm Weitling. There remains, however, in the eyes of Engels, an essential difference between the two movements: the primitive Christians transposed deliverance to the hereafter whereas socialism places it in this world.[10]

But is this difference as clear-cut as it appears at first sight? In his study of the great peasant wars in Germany, it seems to become blurred: Thomas Münzer, the theologian and leader of the revolutionary peasants and heretic (Anabaptist) plebeians of the sixteenth century, wanted the immediate establishment *on earth* of the Kingdom of God, the millenarian Kingdom of the prophets. According to Engels, the Kingdom of God for Münzer was a society without class differences, private property and state authority independent of, or foreign to, the members of that society. However, Engels was still tempted to reduce religion to a stratagem: he spoke of Münzer's Christian 'phraseology' and his biblical 'cloak'.[11] The specifically religious dimension of Münzerian millenarianism – its spiritual and moral force, its authentically experienced mystical depth – seems to have eluded him.

Engels does not hide his admiration for the German chiliastic prophet, whose ideas he describes as 'quasi-communist' and 'religious revolutionary': they were less a synthesis of the plebeian demands from those times than 'a brilliant anticipation' of future proletarian emancipatory aims. This *anticipatory and utopian* dimension of religion – not to be explained in terms of the 'reflection theory' – is not further explored by Engels but is intensely and richly worked out (as we shall see later) by Ernst Bloch.

The last revolutionary movement that was waged under the banner of religion was, according to Engels, the English Puritan movement of the seventeenth century. If religion, not materialism, furnished the ideology of this revolution, it was because of the politically reactionary nature of this philosophy in England, represented by Hobbes and other partisans of royal absolutism. In contrast to this conservative materialism and deism, the Protestant sects gave to the war against the Stuarts its religious banner and its fighters.[12] This analysis is quite interesting: breaking with the linear vision of history inherited from the Enlightenment, Engels acknowledges that the struggle between materialism and religion does not necessarily correspond to the war between revolution and counter-revolution, progress and regression, liberty and despotism, oppressed and ruling classes. In this precise case, the relationship is exactly the opposite: revolutionary religion against absolutist materialism.

Engels was convinced that since the French Revolution religion could no longer function as a revolutionary ideology, and he was surprised when French and German communists – such as Cabet or Weitling – claimed that 'Christianity is Communism'. This disagreement on religion was one of the main reasons for the non-participation of French communists in the *French–German Yearbooks* (1844) and for the split with Weitling in 1846.

Engels could not predict liberation theology, but, thanks to his analysis of the religious phenomena from the viewpoint of class struggle, he brought out the protest potential of religion and opened the way for a new approach – distinct both from Enlightenment philosophy (religion as a clerical conspiracy) and from German neo-Hegelianism (religion as alienated human essence) – to the relationship between religion and society.

Most twentieth-century Marxist studies of religion limit themselves to commenting on or developing the ideas sketched out by Marx and Engels, or to applying them to a particular reality. This was the case with, for example, Karl Kautsky's historical studies of primitive Christianity, medieval heresies, Thomas More and Thomas Münzer. He considered all these religious currents as communist movements and 'forerunners of modern socialism' (that was the title of his series of essays), whose aim was a sort of *distributive communism* – as opposed to the productive communism of the modern labour movement. While Kautsky provides us with interesting insights into and details of the social and economic bases of these movements and their communist aspirations, he usually reduces their religious beliefs to a simple 'envelope' [*Hülle*] or 'garb' [*Gewand*] that 'conceals' their social content. The mystical, apocalyptic and chiliastic manifestations of the medieval heresies are, in his view, nothing but expressions of despair, resulting from the impossibility of accomplishing their communist ideals.[13] In his book on the German Reformation, he wastes no time on the religious dimension of the struggle between Catholics, Lutherans and Anabaptists: despising what he calls the 'theological squabbles' [*theologischen Zänkereien*] between those religious movements, he sees the only task of the historian 'to trace back the fights of those times to the contradictions of material interests'. Luther's 95 Theses are not so much a quarrel about dogmas as a conflict over economic issues: the money-bag [*Geldbeutel*] which Rome extracted from Germany in the form of Church taxes.[14]

Kautsky's book on Thomas More is more original: it gives a glowing and idyllic picture of popular medieval Christianity as a joyful and happy religion, full of vitality and of lively celebrations and feasts. The author of *Utopia* is presented as the last representative of this old, feudal popular Catholicism – quite different from the modern Jesuitical one. According to Kautsky, Thomas More chose Catholicism and not Protestantism as a religion because he was opposed to the forceful proletarianization of the peasants resulting from the destruction of the traditional Church and community land-tenure by the Protestant Reformation in England. On the other hand, the religious institutions of the island 'Utopia' show that Thomas More was far from being a partisan of the established Catholic authoritarianism: he advocated religious tolerance, the abolition of clerical celibacy, the election of priests by their communities, and the ordination of women.[15]

Many Marxists in the European labour movement were radically hostile to religion, but believed that the atheistic battle against religious ideology must be subordinated to the concrete necessities of the class struggle, which demands unity between workers who believe in God and those who do not. Lenin himself, who very often denounced religion as a 'mystical fog', insisted in his article 'Socialism and Religion' (1905) that atheism should not be part of the Party's programme because 'unity in the really revolutionary struggle of the oppressed class for creation of a paradise on earth is more important to us than unity of proletarian opinion on paradise in heaven'.[16]

Rosa Luxemburg shared this strategy, but she developed a

different and original approach. Although she was a staunch atheist herself, in her writings she attacked religion, as such, less than she did the reactionary policy of the Church in the name of its own tradition. In an essay written in 1905 ('Church and Socialism') she claimed that modern socialists are more faithful to the original principles of Christianity than the conservative clergy of today. Since the socialists struggle for a social order of equality, freedom and fraternity, the priests, if they honestly wanted to implement in the life of humanity the Christian principle 'love thy neighbour as thyself', should welcome the socialist movement. When the clergy support the rich, and those who exploit and oppress the poor, they are in explicit contravention of Christian teachings: they serve not Christ but the Golden Calf. The first apostles of Christianity were passionate communists and the Fathers of the Church (like Basil the Great and John Chrysostom) denounced social injustice. Today this cause is taken up by the socialist movement, which brings to the poor the Gospel of fraternity and equality, and calls on the people to establish on earth the Kingdom of Freedom and neighbourly love.[17] Instead of waging a philosophical battle in the name of materialism, Rosa Luxemburg tried to rescue the social dimension of the Christian tradition for the labour movement.

Austrian Marxists, like Otto Bauer and Max Adler, were much less hostile to religion than their German or Russian comrades. They seemed to consider Marxism as compatible with some form of religion, but this referred mainly to religion as a 'philosophical belief' (of neo-Kantian inspiration) rather than to concrete historical religious traditions.[18]

In the Communist International little attention was paid to religion, although a significant number of Christians joined the movement, and a former Swiss Protestant pastor, Jules Humbert-Droz, became, during the 1920s, one of the leading figures of the Comintern. The dominant idea among Marxists at that time was that a Christian who became a socialist or communist necessarily abandoned his former 'anti-scientific' and 'idealist' religious beliefs. Bertold Brecht's beautiful play *Saint Joan of the Stockyards* (1932) is a good example of this kind of approach to the conversion of Christians to the struggle for proletarian emancipation. Brecht describes very perceptively the process by which Joan, a leader of the Salvation Army, discovers the truth about exploitation and social injustice, and dies denouncing her former views. But for him there must be an absolute and total break between her old Christian faith and her new credo of revolutionary struggle. Just before dying, Joan says to the people:

> If ever someone comes to tell you
> that there exists a God, invisible however,
> from whom you can expect help,
> hit him hard in the head with a stone
> until he dies.

Rosa Luxemburg's insight, that one could fight for socialism in the name of the true values of original Christianity, was lost in this kind of crude and somewhat intolerant 'materialist' perspective. As a matter of fact, a few years after Brecht wrote this piece, there appeared in France (1936–38) a movement of revolutionary Christians, numbering several thousand followers, which actively supported the labour movement, in particular its more radical tendencies (the left wing of the Socialist Party). Their main slogan was 'We are socialists because we are Christians'.[19]

Among the leaders and thinkers of the communist movement, Gramsci was probably the one who showed the greatest attention to religious issues. Unlike Engels or Kautsky he was interested not in primitive Christianity or the communist heresies of the Middle Ages but, rather, in the functioning of the *Catholic Church*: he was one of the first Marxists who tried to understand the contemporary role of the Church and the weight of religious culture among the popular masses. In his youthful writings Gramsci shows sympathy for progressive forms of religiosity. For instance, he is fascinated by the Christian socialist Charles Péguy: 'the most obvious characteristic of Péguy's personality is religiosity, the intense faith. . . . His books are all full of this mysticism inspired by the most pure and persuasive enthusiasm, which takes the form of a very personal prose, of Biblical intonation'. Reading Péguy's *Notre Jeunesse*: 'we become drunk with that *mystical religious feeling of socialism*, of justice that pervades everything. . . . We feel in ourselves a new life, a stronger faith beyond the ordinary and miserable polemics of the small and vulgarly materialist politicians'.[20]

Gramsci's most substantial writings on religion, however, are to be found in the *Prison Notebooks*: in spite of their fragmentary, unsystematic and allusive nature, they contain most insightful remarks. His sharp and ironic criticism of the conservative forms of religion – particularly the Jesuitical brand of Catholicism, which he heartily disliked – did not prevent him from perceiving also the utopian dimension of religious ideas:

Religion is the most gigantic utopia, that is, the most gigantic 'metaphysics', that history has ever known, since it is the most grandiose attempt to reconcile, in mythological form, the real contradictions of historical life. It affirms, in fact, that mankind has the same 'nature', that man . . . in so far as created by God, son of God, is therefore brother of other men, equal to other men, and free amongst and as other men . . . ; but it also affirms that all this is not of this world, but of another (the utopia). Thus do ideas of equality, fraternity and liberty ferment among men. . . . Thus it has come about that in every radical stirring of the multitude, in one way or another, with particular forms and particular ideologies, these demands have always been raised.

He also insisted on the internal differentiations of the Church according to ideological orientations – liberal, modernist, Jesuitical and fundamentalist currents within Catholic culture – and according to the different social classes: 'Every religion . . . is really a multiplicity of different and often contradictory religions: there is a Catholicism for the peasants, a Catholicism for the petty bourgeoisie and urban workers, a Catholicism for women, and a Catholicism for intellectuals.' Moreover, he believed that Christianity is, under certain historical conditions, 'a necessary form of the will of the popular masses, a specific form of rationality in the world and of life'; but this applies only to the innocent religion of the people, not to the 'Jesuitical Christianity' [*cristianesimo gesuitizzato*], which is 'pure narcotics for the popular masses'.[21]

Most of Gramsci's notes relate to the history and present role of the Catholic Church in Italy: its social and political expression through Catholic Action and the People's Party, its relation to the State and to the subordinate classes, and so on. While he focused on the class divisions inside the Church, Gramsci was also aware of the relative autonomy of the institution, as a body composed of 'traditional intellectuals' (the clergy and the lay Catholic intellectuals) – that is, intellectuals linked to a feudal past and not 'organically' connected to any modern social class. This is why the main motive for the political actions of the Church, and for its conflictive relation with the Italian bourgeoisie, is the defence of its corporative interests, its power and its privileges.

Gramsci was very much interested by the Protestant Reformation; unlike Engels and Kautsky, however, he focused not on Thomas Münzer and the Anabaptists but, rather, on Luther and Calvin. As an attentive reader of Max Weber's *The Protestant Ethic*, he believed that the transformation of the Calvinistic doctrine of predestination into 'one of the major impulses for practical initiative which took place in the world history', is a classical example of the passage from a world-view into a practical norm of behaviour. To some extent, one can consider that Gramsci used Weber in order to supersede the economistic approach of vulgar Marxism, by focusing on the historically productive role of ideas and representations.[22]

His relation to Protestantism, however, was much broader than this methodological issue: for him the Protestant Reformation, as a truly national/popular movement, able to mobilize the masses, was a sort of paradigm for the great 'moral and intellectual reform' that Marxism seeks to accomplish: the philosophy of praxis 'corresponds to the connexion Protestant Reform + French Revolution: it is a philosophy that is also politics and politics that is also a philosophy'. While Kautsky, living in Protestant Germany, idealized the Italian Renaissance, and despised the Reform as 'barbarian', Gramsci, the Italian Marxist, praised Luther and Calvin, and denounced the Renaissance as an aristocratic and reactionary movement.[23]

Gramsci's remarks are rich and stimulating, but in the last analysis they follow the classical Marxist pattern of analysing religion. Ernst Bloch was the first Marxist author who radically changed the theoretical framework – without abandoning the Marxist and revolutionary perspective. In a similar way to Engels, he distinguished two socially opposed currents: on one side the theocratic religion of the official churches, opium of the people, a mystifying apparatus at the service of the powerful; on the other the underground, subversive and heretical religion of the Albigensians, the Hussites, Joachim di Fiori, Thomas Münzer, Franz von Baader, Wilhelm Weitling and Leo Tolstoy. However, unlike Engels, Bloch refused to see religion uniquely as a 'cloak' of class interests: he explicitly criticized this conception, while attributing it to Kautsky only. In its protest and rebellious forms, religion is one of the most significant forms of *utopian* consciousness, one of the richest expressions of the *principle of hope*. Through its capacity for creative anticipation, Judaeo-Christian eschatology – Bloch's favourite religious universe – contributes to shaping the imaginary space of the *not-yet-being*.[24]

Based on these philosophical presuppositions, Bloch develops a heterodox and iconoclastic interpretation of the Bible – both the Old and the New Testaments – drawing out the *Biblia pauperum*, which denounces the Pharaohs and calls on each and every person to choose *aut Caesar aut Christus*, either Caesar or Christ.

A religious atheist – according to him only an atheist can be a good Christian and vice-versa – and a theologian of the revolution, Bloch produced not only a Marxist reading of millenarianism (following Engels) but also, and this was new, a *millenarian interpretation of Marxism*, through which the socialist struggle for the Kingdom of Freedom is perceived as the direct heir of the eschatological and collectivist heresies of the past.

Of course Bloch, like the young Marx of the famous 1844 quotation, recognized the dual character of the religious phenomenon, its oppressive aspect as well as its potential for revolt. The first requires the use of what he called 'the cold stream of Marxism': the relentless materialist analysis of ideologies, idols and idolatries. The second, however, requires 'the warm stream of Marxism', seeking to rescue religion's *utopian cultural surplus*, its critical and anticipatory force. Beyond any 'dialogue', Bloch dreamt of an authentic union between Christianity and revolution, like the one which came into being during the Peasant Wars of the sixteenth century.

Bloch's views were, to a certain extent, shared by some of the members of the Frankfurt School. Max Horkheimer considered that 'religion is the record of the wishes, nostalgias (*Sehnsüchte*) and indictments of countless generations'.[25] Erich Fromm, in his book, *The Dogma of Christ* (1930), used Marxism and psychoanalysis to illuminate the messianic, plebeian, egalitarian and anti-authoritarian essence of primitive Christianity. And Walter Benjamin tried to combine, in a unique and original synthesis, theology and Marxism, Jewish messianism and historical materialism, class struggle and redemption.[26]

Lucien Goldmann's work is another path-breaking attempt at renewing the Marxist study of religion. Although he was of a very different inspiration from Bloch, he was also interested in redeeming the moral and human values of religious tradition. In his book *The Hidden God* (1955) he developed a very subtle and inventive sociological analysis of the Jansenist heresy (including Racine's theatre and Pascal's philosophy) as a tragic world-view, expressing the peculiar situation of a social layer (the *noblesse de robe*) in seventeenth-century France. One of his methodological innovations was to relate religion not only to the interests of the class, but to its whole *existential condition*: he therefore examined how this legal and administrative layer, torn between its dependency on, and its opposition to, the absolute monarchy, gave a religious expression to its dilemmas in the tragic world-view of Jansenism. According to David McLellan, this is the 'most impressive specific analysis of religion produced by Western Marxism'.[27]

The most surprising and original part of the work is, however, the attempt to compare – without assimilating one to another – *religious faith* and *Marxist faith*: both have in common the refusal of pure individualism (rationalist or empiricist) and the belief in *trans-individual values* – God for religion, the human community for socialism. In both cases the faith is based on a wager – the Pascalian wager on the existence of God and the Marxist wager on the liberation of humanity – that presupposes risk, the danger of failure and the hope of success. Both imply some fundamental belief which is not demonstrable on the exclusive level of factual judgements. What separates them is, of course, the supra-historical character of religious transcendence: 'The Marxist faith is a faith in the historical future that human beings themselves make, or rather that we must make by our activity, a "wager" on the success of our actions; the transcendence that is the object of this faith is neither supernatural nor trans-historical, but supra-individual, nothing more but also nothing less.'[28] Without wanting in any way to 'christianize Marxism', Lucien Goldmann introduced, thanks to the concept of *faith*, a new way of looking at the conflictual relationship between religious belief and Marxist atheism.

The idea that common ground exists between the revolutionary and the religious mind had already been suggested, in a less systematic way, by the most original and creative Latin American Marxist, the Peruvian José Carlos Mariátegui. In an essay of 1925, 'Man and the Myth', he proposed a rather heterodox view of revolutionary values:

> The bourgeois intellectuals busy themselves with a rationalist critique of the revolutionary's method, theory and technique. What a misunderstanding! The force of the revolutionaries does not lie in their science; it lies in their faith, their passion, their will. It's a religious, mystical, spiritual force. It is the force of Myth. . . . The revolutionary emotion . . . is a religious emotion. The religious motivations have moved from heaven to earth. They are no more divine, but human and social.

Celebrating Georges Sorel as the first Marxist thinker who understood the 'religious, mystical, metaphysical character of socialism', he wrote a few years later, in his last book, *Defence of Marxism* (1930):

> Thanks to Sorel, Marxism was able to assimilate the substantive elements and acquisitions of the philosophical currents that came after Marx. Superseding the rationalist and positivist bases of the socialism at his time, Sorel found in Bergson and the pragmatists ideas that strengthened socialist thought, restoring it to its revolutionary mission. . . . The theory of revolutionary myths, applying to the socialist movement the experience of the religious movements, established the basis for a philosophy of revolution.'[29]

This formulation – expression of a Romantic/Marxist rebellion against the dominant (semi-positivist) interpretation of historical materialism – may seem too radical. In any case, it should be clear that Mariátegui did not want to make of socialism a Church or a religious sect, but intended to bring out the spiritual and ethical dimension of the revolutionary struggle: the faith ('mystical'), the solidarity, the moral indignation, the total commitment at the risk of one's own life (what he called the 'heroic'). Socialism for Mariátegui was inseparable from an attempt to re-enchant the world through revolutionary action. Little wonder that he became one of the most important Marxist references for the founder of liberation theology, the Peruvian Gustavo Gutiérrez.

Marx and Engels thought religion's subversive role was a thing of the past, which no longer had any significance in the epoch of modern class struggle. This forecast was more or less historically confirmed for a century – with a few important exceptions (particularly in France): the Christian socialists of the 1930s, the worker priests of the 1940s, the left wing of the Christian unions (the Confédération Française des Travailleurs Chrétiens) in the 1950s, etc. But to understand what has been happening for the last thirty years in Latin America (and to a lesser extent also in other continents) around the issue of *liberation theology* we need to integrate into our analysis the insights of Bloch and Goldmann on the utopian potential of the Judaeo-Christian tradition.

Catholic Ethics and the Spirit of Capitalism:
The Unwritten Chapter in Max Weber's
Sociology of Religion

The main argument of Max Weber's *The Protestant Ethic and the Spirit of Capitalism* is not so much (as is often said) that religion is the determinant causal factor of economic development, but rather that there exists between certain religious forms and the capitalist lifestyle a relationship of *elective affinity* [*Wahlverwandtschaft*]. Weber does not define what he means by this term, but one can deduce from his writings that it designates a relationship of mutual attraction and mutual reinforcement, leading, in certain cases, to a sort of cultural symbiosis.[30]

What about the economic significance of Catholic ethics? Max Weber never wrote a systematic assessment of the relations between Catholicism and the capitalist ethos, but there is an obvious 'subtext', an unwritten counter-argument built into the very structure of *The Protestant Ethic*: the Catholic Church is a much less favourable – if not downright hostile – environment for the development of capitalism than the Calvinist and Methodist sects. Why is it so? In fact, there are some insights, both in this book and in some of his other works, that constitute a sort of (partial) answer to this question. Although these arguments are dispersed in different writings and were never developed or systematized by Weber, they give us some very precious clues to understanding the tension between Catholicism and capitalism. Curiously enough, there is – as far as I know – practically no substantial treatment of this issue in the immense literature written around the Weberian thesis published in the last eighty years. Let us try to reconstruct this unwritten Weberian essay, by using all his references to this tension, and then verify his hypothesis in the light of some other historical or religious sources.

Paradoxically, *The Protestant Ethic* is one of Weber's writings that has little to say about this issue. Although the first chapter deals extensively with the differences in economic development between the predominantly Catholic and the mainly Protestant areas in Germany, there is little attempt to examine the barriers to capitalist growth imposed by the Catholic culture. He limits himself to mentioning 'St. Thomas's characterization of the desire for gain as *turpitudo* (which term even included the unavoidable and hence ethically justified profit-making)'. In a more explicit passage, he argues that in the Catholic tradition 'the feeling was never quite overcome, that activity directed to acquisition for its own sake was at bottom a *pudendum* which was to be tolerated only because of the unalterable necessities of life in this world. . . . The dominant doctrine rejected the spirit of capitalist acquisition as *turpitudo*, or at least could not give it a positive ethical sanction.'[31]

In the debate that followed the publication of the book, Weber suggested a new idea: the *incompatibility* [*Unvereinbarkeit*] between the ideals of the serious Catholic believer and the 'commercial' struggle for acquisition; but he did not mention any ethical or religious reasons for this opposition.[32]

It is only several years later, in the 'Zwischenbetrachtung' (1915–16), that we find some – very interesting – explanatory hypotheses. At first Weber does not deal specifically with Catholicism, but with the general tension between the soteriological ethics of fraternity and the values of the world: an *irreconcilable split* [*unversöhlicher zwiespalt*] that is nowhere so visible as in the economic sphere, where sublimated redemptive religiosity clashes with the rationalized economy, based on money, the market, and competition, as well as abstract and impersonal calculation: 'The more the cosmos of the modern rational capitalist economy follows its own immanent inner laws, the less it is accessible to any imaginable relation to a religious ethics of fraternity. . . . Formal and substantive rationality stay here in a mutual conflict.'

Interestingly enough, Weber does not present religious ethics as irrational in opposition to the rational economic (capitalist) system, but describes both as two different sorts of rationality, in terms ('formal and substantive') that are not too far from those later used by the Frankfurt School ('instrumental and substantive').

The main example – mentioned in the 'Zwischenbetrachtung' – of such religious mistrust of the rise of impersonal economic forces, necessarily hostile to the ethics of fraternity [*brüderlich-keitsfeindliche ökonomischen Mächte*], is the Catholic Church: 'The Catholic "*Deo placere non potest*" was durably characteristic of its attitude towards economic life'. Of course, the Church was forced, by its own dependence on economic activities, to compromise, as one can see, for instance, in the history of the ban on loan-interest [*Zinsverbot*]. However, 'in the last instance, the tension itself could hardly be overcome'.[33]

The issue is once more taken up – and the analysis deepened – in *Economy and Society*. This time Weber directly discusses the relation between Catholic ethics and capitalism. Referring to the long and obstinate fight of the Catholic Church against interest rates, he speaks of a 'principled struggle between the ethical and the economical rationalization of the economy', whose motivations he describes as follows:

> Above all, it is the unpersonal, economically rational, but consequently, ethically irrational character of pure business [*geschäftlicher*] relationships as such, that gives rise, precisely among ethical religions, to such a feeling of mistrust, which is never made explicit, but the more so deeply felt. Each purely personal relation of human being to human being, whatever it may be, including the most complete slavery, can be ethically regulated, and ethical norms can be posited, since its structure depends on the individual wills of the participants, and therefore there is room for the deployment of charitable virtues. Not so, however, with rational business relations, and the less so, the more they are rationally differentiated. . . . The reification [*Versachlichung*] of the economy on the basis of the socialization by the market follows entirely its own objectified [*sachlichen*] laws. . . . The reified universe [*versachlichte Kosmos*] of capitalism offers finally no room for any charitable orientation. . . . Therefore, in a characteristic ambiguity, the clergy has always supported – also in the interests of traditionalism – patriarchalism against impersonal relations of dependence, although, on the other hand, prophecy breaks down patriarchal links.[34]

This is an extremely insightful analysis, which helps us to understand both the opposition of Latin American progressive Catholics to the cold and impersonal nature of capitalist relations *and* their struggle, in the name of prophetic justice, against traditional patriarchal domination over peasant communities. While it has taken, as we shall see, an entirely new form, this movement has deep roots in that double (or 'ambiguous') Catholic tradition.

Weber strongly emphasizes the moral hostility of the Church towards the abstract and reified logic of the capitalist system in his *Economic History*. Referring to the paradox that capitalism emerged in the West, i.e. in a part of the world where the dominant ideology had 'an economic theory entirely hostile to capital' [*durchhaus kapitalfeindliche Wirtschaftstheorie*], he added the following commentary:

> The ethos of the Church's economic ethics is summarized in its judgement, probably taken up from Arianism, about the merchant: *homo mercator vix aut numquam potest Deo placere*. . . . The deep aversion [*Abneigung*] of the Catholic and following it the Lutheran ethics to any

capitalist initiative is essentially grounded in fear of the impersonal nature of relations inside a capitalist economy. This impersonality is the reason why certain human relations are torn away from the Church and its influence, and why it becomes impossible for it to ethically penetrate or shape them.[35]

One of the consequences of this 'deep division between the economic inevitable requirements and the Christian ideal of life' was the 'ethical downgrading' of the rational economic spirit.[36] It is to be noted that Weber associates in a common opposition to the capitalist ethos both the Catholic and the Lutheran ethics – a somewhat different approach from the one in *The Protestant Ethic*, although in the earlier work a distinction was already made between the Lutheran and the Calvinist or Methodist form of Protestantism which was considered the most favourable for the development of capitalist accumulation.

In any case, Weber hints at the existence of an essential and irreconcilable aversion to or rejection of the spirit of capitalism by the Catholic Church (and probably also some Protestant denominations). One could speak of a sort of cultural *antipathy* – in the old, alchemical meaning of the word: 'lack of affinity between two substances'. In other words, we have here an exact inversion of the *elective affinity* [*Wahlverwandtschaft*] between (some forms of) the Protestant ethic and the spirit of capitalism: there would exist, between the Catholic ethic and capitalism, a sort of *negative affinity* – using this term much as Weber does when he speaks of the 'negative privileges' of pariah communities.

As Weber himself hints, this does not prevent a 'realistic' accommodation and adaptation of the Catholic institutions to the capitalist system, particularly as it grows increasingly powerful; the Church's criticism is usually directed against the excesses of liberalism rather than against the foundations of capitalism. Moreover, confronted with a much greater danger – the socialist labour movement – the Church did not hesitate to join forces with bourgeois and capitalist forces against this common enemy. In general it can be said that the Church never thought it possible or desirable to abolish capitalism: its aim was always to correct its most negative aspects by the charitable and 'social' action of Christianity. But there remains, deeply ingrained in Catholic culture – sometimes hidden, sometimes manifest – the ethical aversion to, or 'negative affinity' with, capitalism.

How far does historical investigation confirm or deny this –

rather implicit – Weberian hypothesis? It would be beyond the scope of this chapter to discuss the issue at any length. Let us only mention a few important studies that seem to support this contention. For instance, the evidence provided by Bernard Groethuysen, in his well-known work on the origins of bourgeois society in France (*The Bourgeois: Catholicism vs. Capitalism in Eighteenth-Century France*), strongly highlights the Church's opposition to the rise of capitalism. Drawing extensively on the writings of Catholic theologians of the seventeenth and eighteenth centuries, such as Father Thomassin's *Traité du négoce et de l'usure* (1697) or Pierre Bayle's well-known *Dictionnaire historique et critique* (1695), he points to their systematic anti-capitalist and anti-bourgeois bias:

> Thus a whole class of society was the target. It was not the newly rich or the rich in general . . . that the ministers of God attacked; it was the big industrialists, the big bankers, the merchant contractors, to whom they pointed by name. . . . They were all classed as 'capitalists' and 'usurers', as men who deliberately ignored the commandments of God.

It should be stressed, however, that unlike Weber's supposition, it is not so much the impersonality of the new economic system as its injustice that motivates most of the moral outrage (although the two are not necessarily contradictory), as in this typical passage from Prigent's *Observations sur le prêt à interêt dans le commerce* (1783):

> Industry's capital is multiplied, but for whose benefit? For that of the artisans who give of their labour? Most of them have only work, poverty and abasement as their lot. The funds which are accumulated are poured into the coffers of a small number of businessmen, fattened on the sweat of a host of workers who wear themselves out in dismal manufacture.[37]

Groethuysen's research, and the work of several other historians, points to a source of Catholic anti-capitalism that Weber seemed to neglect: the ethical and religious identification of Christ with the poor (inspired by Matthew 25: 31). For centuries, Catholic theology and popular tradition saw the poor as the earthly image of Christ's sufferings. As the theologian A. Bonnefous wrote in his book *Le Chrestien charitable* (1637), 'the poor man one helps is perhaps Jesus Christ himself'.[38] Of course, this attitude led mainly to charitable attention to the poor, without necessarily rejecting the existing economic system. However, it also nourished, during the whole history of the Church, rebel movements and doctrines that challenged social injustice in the name of the poor, and, in modern times, denounced capitalism as the root of the evil and the cause of impoverishment. This is particularly true of liberation theology in Latin America, as we shall see.

A similar analysis to Groethuysen's is presented, for the nineteenth and early twentieth centuries, by Émile Poulat, in his book *The Church against the Bourgeoisie. An introduction to the origins of present social Catholicism*. Using mainly Italian sources, Poulat describes a broad European tendency that he calls *intransigent Catholicism*, whose influence explains the persistent opposition of the Church to modern bourgeois civilization. Although intransigent Catholicism is also radically hostile to socialism, 'both declare themselves to be incompatible with the spirit of liberalism that pervades bourgeois society and the capitalist economy'. Voices pleading, like that of the French Catholic author Émile de Laveleye in 1888, for 'an alliance of Catholicism and socialism against the liberal bourgeoisie, their common enemy', were quite isolated.[39]

There have not been equivalent studies on the history of Latin American Catholicism, but recently, in a brilliant essay on the Catholic baroque ethos of the Hispanic-American culture of the seventeenth and eighteenth centuries, the Mexican scholar Bolivar Echevarría argued that this was a historical world 'connected to the attempt by the Catholic Church to build a religious form of modernity, based on the revitalization of faith – as an alternative to the abstract individualistic modernity, which was grounded in the vitality of capital.'[40]

Modern Catholic thinkers have used both Weber's (for the Protestant aspect) and Groethuysen's works to argue that 'the Catholic ethos is anti-capitalistic'. This statement appears in Amintore Fanfani's book *Catholicism, Protestantism and Capitalism* (1935). Following Weber, the author – at that time a young Catholic intellectual, later to become a leader of the Christian Democratic Party and Italy's prime minister – defines capitalism as a system of economic rationalization that is impermeable to exterior influences. The following conclusion results from this premiss:

> To discover a principle on which to base criticism of a system like capitalism within that system is impossible. Criticism can only come from another order of ideas, from a system that would direct social

activity towards non-capitalistic aims. This Catholicism does when its social ethics demand that ends must converge in a definitely non-capitalistic direction.

Moreover,

> in an age in which the Catholic conception of life had a real hold over the mind, capitalist action could only have manifested itself as something erroneous, reprehensible, spasmodic, and sinful, to be condemned by the faith and knowledge of the agent himself. . . . The anti-capitalistic action of the Church, which was very intensive in the fifteenth and sixteenth centuries, was still, as Groethuysen has pointed out, in full force in eighteenth century.[41]

According to Fanfani, while Protestantism favoured the dominance of the capitalist spirit, or rather, legitimized it and sanctified it – Weber's thesis reviewed and corrected by H.M. Robertson – 'there is an unbridgeable gulf between the Catholic and the capitalist conception of life'. In order to understand this difference, one has to take into consideration the fact that, unlike the Protestant ethic, 'in their general lines, Catholic social ethics are always antithetical to capitalism'. As a result of this contradiction, Catholicism shows a 'most decided repugnance' towards capitalism – not against this or that aspect (nearly all such aspects being accidental) but against the essence itself of the system.[42]

Of course, not all Catholic intellectuals shared such a radical viewpoint, and the author himself, Amintore Fanfani, was to become a typical manager of the capitalist economy as Italy's prime minister after the war. However, the book became, according to a new preface written in 1984 by Michael Novak, 'a *locus classicus* of anti-capitalist sentiment among Catholic intellectuals'.

Michael Novak, the well-known US religious neo-conservative, is a good example of pro-capitalist Catholic thinking. However, his innumerable complaints against what he calls 'the Catholic anti-capitalist bias', his open dissatisfaction with what he considers to be a serious short-coming of his own religious tradition, constitute another piece of evidence, albeit involuntary, for the existence of a sort of *negative affinity*, or *cultural antipathy*, between the Catholic ethic and the spirit of capitalism. According to Novak, a book like Fanfani's:

> helps to explain why Catholic nations were long retarded in encouraging development, invention, savings, investment, entrepreneurship, and, in general, economic dynamism. In the name of Catholic ideals it is blind

to its own prejudices. It fails to state correctly the capitalist ideal. It fails also to see some of the faults and the underdeveloped parts in Catholic social thought.[43]

Similar criticism of 'the Catholic anti-capitalist tradition', and of the Catholic 'bias against democratic capitalism', can also be found in Novak's main works, such as the much-celebrated apologetic piece *The Spirit of Democratic Capitalism* (1982). According to the author, Catholic attitudes towards money were 'based on premodern realities' and Catholic thought 'did not understand the creativity and productivity of wisely invested capital'; fascinated with distributive ethics, it has 'misread the liberal democratic capitalist revolution', particularly in Great Britain and the United States.[44]

Novack accused the Catholic Church of being too conservative. It is true that this Catholic anti-capitalist bias, this hostility towards modern bourgeois society has had, since its origin, an overwhelmingly conservative, restorative, regressive – in a word, *reactionary* – tendency. It clearly expressed the Church's nostalgia for the feudal/corporative past, for a pre-capitalist hierarchical society in which it had outstanding power and privileges. It very often took the sinister form of *anti-Semitism*, the Jew serving as a scapegoat for the evils of usury, the dissolving power of money and the rise of capitalism. However, next to this dominant orientation – and in a more or less conflictual relation to it – there also existed a different Catholic sensibility, whose main motivation was sympathy with the plight of the poor, and which was – to some extent at least – attracted by the socialist or communist utopias. Of course, the two dimensions are not always contradictory, and between the opposite poles of progressive utopia and regressive restoration, there exists a whole spectrum of ambiguous, ambivalent or intermediary positions. Although Weber was mainly interested in the (mostly negative) consequences of Catholic ethics for the rise and growth of a modern industrial economy, one can easily show that the same sort of religious anti-capitalism inspired the active commitment of Catholics to the social emancipation of the poor.

The first modern example of such a utopian Catholicism is that of Thomas More, who not only dreamt of a sort of 'communist' system (quite authoritarian, by the way) but also denounced one of the key aspects of what Marx defined as the primitive accumulation of capital in the sixteenth century: the enclosures that expelled the poor peasants from their land and replaced them by sheep ('sheep, which are normally so gentle . . . have begun to be so ravenous and wild that they even eat up men'). Condemning the 'pernicious pests' who stripped the tenants of their lands by trickery or violence, and the 'wicked greed of a few', Thomas More lamented the 'wretched poverty' of most of the English people and called for a new economic policy: 'Check the rich from buying everything up and put an end to their freedom of monopoly'.[45]

We cannot follow here the evolution of the conservative and the utopian currents in Catholic (or Protestant) anti-capitalism throughout the centuries. Let us just recall that, at the begining of the nineteenth century, we can find a strange combination of both in what Marx ironically called feudal or Christian socialism: 'half lamentation, half lampoon; half echo of the past, half menace of the future; at times, by its bitter, witty and incisive criticism, striking the bourgeoisie to the very heart's core; but always ludicrous in its effect, through total incapacity to comprehend the march of modern history'.[46] He was perhaps referring to authors like the Romantic Catholic social philosopher Johannes von Baader, a staunch partisan of Church and King, who denounced the miserable condition of the *proletairs* (his term) in England and France as more cruel and inhuman than serfdom. Criticizing the brutal and unchristian exploitation of this propertyless class by the moneyed interests [*Argyrokratie*], he suggested that the Catholic clergy should become the advocate and representative of the *proletairs*.[47]

Johannes von Baader is representative of a distinctive Catholic form of Romantic culture. Romanticism is much more than a literary school: it constitutes a world-view that embraces all spheres of culture. One could define it as a protest against modern capitalist/industrial civilization in the name of pre-capitalist values, a nostalgic *Weltanschauung* opposed to certain key components of this civilization: disenchantment with the world, quantification of values, mechanization, dissolution of community, abstract rationality. From the late eighteenth century (Rousseau) to the present day, it has been one of the main structures-of-sensibility in modern culture, under various forms, ranging from utter conservatism to revolutionary utopianism. While in the early nineteenth century Catholic thinkers usually belonged to the traditionalist and reactionary part of the Romantic spectrum (with some exceptions, such as the famous abbot Lammennais), this began to change at the begining of the twentieth century, with the emergence of a small current of Catholic socialism.[48]

When writing *The Magic Mountain* shortly after World War I, Thomas Mann represented Catholic Romantic culture, with all its ambiguities, in the strange figure of Leon Naphta, a revolutionary Jesuit, a fervent partisan of the medieval Church, and at the same time an apocalyptic prophet of world communism. There is much of Thomas Mann himself in Leon Naphta, but by making him a Jesuit of Jewish origin he was perhaps taking his inspiration from some Jewish-German Romantic revolutionaries, fascinated by medieval Catholic culture. Among this group of 'Gothic socialists' one might include Georg Lukács (who is often presented as the model for the Naphta figure), Gustav Landauer and Ernst Bloch. For all of them the attraction of Gothic culture was intimately related to their Romantic aversion to the modern capitalist/industrial civilization.

Interestingly enough, several of these utopian authors used Max Weber's work to denounce Protestantism and to celebrate medieval Catholic civilization – quite against the intentions of the author of *The Protestant Ethic*. Ernst Bloch, for instance, insisted in *Thomas Münzer, Theologian of Revolution* (1921) on the role of Calvinist innerworldly asceticism in the accumulation of capital. Thanks to the Protestant ethic, 'as Max Weber has brilliantly shown, the emerging capitalist economy was entirely liberated, detached and emancipated from all the scruples of primitive Christianity, as well as from all that remained relatively Christian in the ideology of the Middle Ages'.[49]

Paradoxically, the upsurge of a Catholic Left seems to be related to the Church's increasing willingness to compromise with bourgeois society. After its bitter condemnation of liberal principles and modern society in the *Syllabus* (1864), Rome seemed to accept, by the end of the nineteenth century, the advent of capitalism and of the modern ('liberal') bourgeois state as irreversible facts. The most visible manifestation of this new strategy is the 'rallying' of the French Church (until then an outspoken supporter of monarchy) to the French Republic. Intransigent Catholicism takes the form of 'social Catholicism', which, while still criticizing the excesses of 'liberal capitalism', does not really challenge the existing social and economic order. This applies to all documents of the so-called Roman magistracy (the papal encyclicals) as well as to the social doctrine of the Church, from *Rerum Novarum* (1891) to the present day.

It was precisely at the moment of the Church's (real or apparent) 'reconciliation' with the modern world that a new form of Catholic socialism emerged, mainly in France, which became a significant minority factor in French Catholic culture. At the turn of the century one sees the simultaneous upsurge of the most reactionary forms of Catholic anti-capitalism – Charles Maurras, the Action Française movement and the regressive wing of the Church, all active in the ugly anti-Semitic campaign against Dreyfus – and of an equally 'intransigent' but now leftist form of anti-capitalism, whose first representative was the philo-Semitic Dreyfusard leader and socialist writer, Charles Péguy, who became a Catholic in 1907, although he never joined the Church. This current was not without its ambiguities (in relation to 'revolutionary conservatism'), but its basic commitment was to the Left.

Few socialist authors have developed a more thorough, radical and vitriolic critique of modern bourgeois society, the spirit of capitalist accumulation, and the impersonal logic of money than Charles Péguy. He is the founder of a specifically French tradition of progressive Christian anti-capitalism (mainly Catholic, but occasionally ecumenical), which has unfolded during the twentieth century, including such diverse figures as: Emmanuel Mounier and his group (the journal *Esprit*), the (small) movement of Revolutionary Christians at the time of the Popular Front, the anti-fascist Resistance network Témoignage Chrétien during World War II, the Worker Priests during the 1940s and the 1950s, the various Christian movements and networks that took part in the foundation, in the late 1950s, of the left-socialist PSU (Parti Socialiste Unifié), the majority current of the Christian Confederation of Labour (CFTC) which became socialist and transformed itself into the Democratic Confederation of Labour (CFDT), as well as a large part of Catholic Youth – students (JEC, JUC) – or workers (JOC) – who actively sympathized, in the 1960s and 1970s, with various socialist, communist or revolutionary movements. To this wide spectrum one has also to add a large number of religious (particularly Dominican) authors and theologians who have shown, since World War II, a great interest in Marxism and socialism: Henri Desroche, Jean-Yves Calvez, M.D. Chenu, Jean Cardonnel, Paul Blanquart, and many others.

The most influential of these figures was probably Emmanuel Mounier: following in the footsteps of Charles Péguy (on whose legacy he wrote one of his first books), he impressed his readers by his passionate critique of capitalism as a system grounded in the 'imperialism of money', the anonymity of the market (we find here the element emphasized by Weber) and the negation of human personality; an ethical and religious aversion that led him to propose an alternative form of society, 'personalist socialism', which has, in his own terms, 'enormously to learn from Marxism'.[50]

Although Christian socialists linked to the Catholic Church can be found elsewhere, there is (outside Latin America) no other such broad and extended religious leftist anti-capitalist tradition as in the French Catholic culture. To examine the reasons for this particularity is beyond the scope of these pages. But it is no accident that the first manifestation of a *progressive Christianity* in Latin America, the so-called Brazilian Christian Left of 1960–62 – whose main advocate was the Catholic Student Union (JUC) – was directly linked to this French culture. To mention just one example: according to the Jesuit Henrique de Vaz Lima, adviser to the JUC, at the begining of the 1960s, Emmanuel Mounier was 'the most influential of Brazilian Catholic youth'.[51]

Latin America's 'Church of the Poor' is the inheritor of the ethical rejection of capitalism by Catholicism – the 'negative affinity' – and especially of this French and European tradition of Christian socialism. When, at a meeting in 1968, the Brazilian JOC (Workers' Catholic Youth) approved a resolution stating that 'capitalism is intrinsically evil, because it prevents the integral development of human beings and the development of solidarity among the people', it gave a most radical and striking expression to this tradition. At the same time, by ironically reversing the well-known formula of papal excommunication of communism as an 'intrinsically perverse system', it dissociated itself from the conservative ('reactionary') aspect of the Church's official doctrine.[52]

In a similar way Herbert José de Souza, one of the main leaders of the Brazilian JUC, paid homage in an article of 1962 to the (official) Catholic anti-capitalist ethos:

> We don't say anything new. We repeat, with all the Popes, the condemnation of capitalism, the need for a more just and human structure, in which social propriety takes the place of the private property of the liberal structure. . . . It is not an accident that all the official documents of the Church condemn capitalism: it is a system that establishes, by principle, inequality of opportunity.[53]

This sort of statement should not be taken too literally: in fact,

Latin American liberationist Christianity is not just a continuation of the Church's traditional anti-capitalism, or of its French Catholic/leftist variant. It is essentially the creation of a new religious culture, expressing the specific conditions of Latin America: dependent capitalism, massive poverty, institutionalized violence, popular religiosity. I shall examine the main aspects of this new culture in the ensuing chapters.

2

Liberationist Christianity in Latin America

Liberation Theology and Liberationist Christianity

What is liberation theology?

First of all, liberation theology is a body of writings produced since 1970 by Latin American figures like Gustavo Gutiérrez (Peru), Rubem Alves, Hugo Assmann, Carlos Mesters, Leonardo and Clodovis Boff, Frei Betto (Brazil), Jon Sobrino, Ignacio Ellacuría (El Salvador), Segundo Galilea, Ronaldo Muñoz (Chile), Pablo Richard (Chile – Costa Rica), José Miguez Bonino, Juan Carlos Scannone, Ruben Dri (Argentina), Enrique Dussel (Argentina – Mexico), Juan-Luis Segundo (Uruguay), Samuel Silva Gotay (Puerto Rico), to name only some of the best known.

However, as Leonardo Boff has stated, liberation theology is the reflection of, and a reflection on, a previous praxis. More precisely, it is the expression of a vast social movement that emerged at the beginning of the 1960s, well before the new theological writings. This movement involves significant sectors of the Church (priests, religious orders, bishops), lay religious movements (Catholic Action, Christian University Youth, Young Christian Workers), popularly based pastoral networks, ecclesiastic base communities (CEBs), as well as several popular organizations created by CEB activists: women's clubs, neighbourhood associations, peasant or workers' unions, etc. Without the existence of this social movement, we could not understand social and historical phenomena of such importance as the emergence of a new workers' movement in Brazil and the rise of the revolution in Central America (as well as, more recently, Chiapas).

Usually this broad social/religious movement is referred to as 'liberation theology', but this is inadequate, in so far as the movement appeared many years before the new theology and most of its activists are hardly theologians at all; sometimes it is also referred to as the 'Church of the Poor', but this social network goes well beyond the limits of the Church as an institution, however broadly defined. I propose to call it *liberationist Christianity*, this being a wider concept than either 'theology' or 'Church', including both the religious culture and the social network, faith and praxis. To say that it is a social movement does not necessarily mean that it is an 'integrated' and 'well-co-ordinated' body, but only that it has, like other such movements (feminism, ecology, etc), a certain capacity for mobilizing people around common aims.[1]

Aspects of 'church' and 'sect' (according to Troeltsch's sociological concepts) can be found in liberationist Christianity. But more insight can be achieved by using the Weberian ideal-type of the 'soteriological communitarian religiosity' [*soteriologische Gemeindereligiosität*], based on an all-embracing ethic of brotherliness [*Brüderlichkeitethik*], whose origins can be traced to old economic forms of neighbourliness ethics.[2] As we shall see later, all these elements can be found, in almost 'pure' form, in the ecclesiastic base communities and popular pastorals in Latin America.

Liberationist Christianity is vigorously opposed by the Vatican and by the ruling body of the Church hierarchy in Latin America – the CELAM (Latin American Bishops' Council) led, since the early 1970s, by the conservative wing of the Church. Can we say that there is a 'class struggle inside the Church'? Yes and no. Yes, to the extent that certain positions correspond to the interests of the ruling elites and others to those of the oppressed. No, to the extent that the bishops, Jesuits or priests who head the 'Church of the Poor' are not themselves poor. Their rallying to the cause of the exploited is motivated by spiritual and moral reasons inspired by their religious culture, Christian faith and Catholic tradition. Furthermore, this moral and religious dimension is an essential factor in the motivation of thousands of Christian activists in the trade unions, neighbourhood associations, base communities and revolutionary fronts. The poor themselves become conscious of their condition and organize to struggle as Christians, belonging to a Church and inspired by a faith. If we look upon this faith and religious identity deeply rooted in popular culture only as an 'envelope' or 'cloak' of social and economic interests, we fall into the sort of reductionist approach which prevents us from understanding the richness and authenticity of the real movement.

Liberation theology is the spiritual product (the term comes, as we know, from Marx's *German Ideology*) of this social movement, but in legitimating it, in providing it with a coherent religious doctrine, it has contributed enormously to its extension and reinforcement. Now, in order to avoid misunderstanding and reductionism (sociological or other) let us recall first of all that liberation theology is not a social and political discourse but, before anything else, a religious and spiritual reflection. As Gustavo Gutiérrez stressed in his pioneering book *Liberation Theology – Perspectives*:

> The first task of the Church is to celebrate in joy the gift of the redemptive action of God in humanity, which accomplished itself through the death and resurrection of Christ. It is the Eucharist, memorial and thanksgiving. Memorial for Christ which supposes an always renewed acceptance of the meaning of life: the total gift to others.[3]

What changes – very deeply – in relation to the Church's tradition is the concrete meaning that it takes from this 'total gift to others'. If one had to summarize in one single formula the central idea of liberation theology, one could refer to the expression consecrated by the Puebla Conference of the Latin American Bishops (1979): 'the preferential option for the poor'. But one must immediately add that, for the new theology, these poor are the agents of their own liberation and the subject of their own history – and not simply, as in the traditional doctrine of the Church, the object of charitable attention.

The full recognition of the poor's human dignity and the special historical and religious mission attributed to them by liberationist Christianity is certainly one of the reasons for its relative success – in some countries at least – in enlisting the support of the poorest layers of society. The motives for this can be better understood by referring to a most remarkable ideal-typical analysis proposed by Max Weber in his study of the economic ethics of the world religions:

> The sense of dignity of socially repressed strata or of strata whose status is negatively (or at least not positively) valued is nourished most easily on the belief that a special 'mission' is entrusted to them; their worth is guaranteed or constituted by an *ethical imperative* . . . Their value is thus moved into something beyond themselves, into a 'task'

placed before them by God. One source of the ideal power of ethical prophecies among socially disadvantaged strata lies in this fact. Resentment has not been required as a leverage; the rational interest in material and ideal compensations as such has been perfectly sufficient.[4]

Whatever the differences between liberation theologians, several basic tenets can be found in most of their writings, which constitute radical innovations. Some of the most important are:

1. The fight against idolatry (not atheism) as the main enemy of religion – that is, against the new idols of death adored by the new Pharaohs, the new Caesars and the new Herods: Mammon, Wealth, the Market, National Security, the State, Military Force, 'Western Christian Civilization'.

2. Historical human liberation as the anticipation of the final salvation in Christ, the Kingdom of God.

3. A critique of traditional dualist theology as the product of Platonic Greek philosophy, and not of the biblical tradition in which human and divine history are distinct but inseparable.

4. A new reading of the Bible, giving significant attention to passages such as Exodus, which is seen as a paradigm of an enslaved people's struggle for liberation.

5. A sharp moral and social indictment of dependent capitalism as an unjust and iniquitous system, as a form of *structural sin*.

6. The use of Marxism as a social-analytical instrument in order to understand the causes of poverty, the contradictions of capitalism and the forms of class struggle.

7. The preferential option for the poor and solidarity with their struggle for self-liberation.

8. The development of Christian base communities among the poor as a new form of Church and as an alternative to the individualist way of life imposed by the capitalist system.

How do religion and politics relate in this sort of movement? As Daniel Levine has pointed out in his recent works, the theories of 'modernization' – which suppose an increasing functional specialization and institutional differentiation between religion and politics – are out of touch with reality in the continent. Such a model of interpretation would work only if 'religion' could be reduced to cult and 'politics' to government. However, in Latin America both have a much broader meaning, and, even if they remain autonomous, a genuinely dialectical link develops between them. Concepts such as 'pastoral work' or 'liberation' have both a religious and a political, a spiritual and a material, a Christian and a social meaning.[5]

We are confronted here with the kind of phenomena described by the French sociologist Henri Desroche as the 'mutual reactivations of the messianic and the revolutionary spirit'.[6] But instead of 'amalgamation' or 'complicity' (terms employed by Desroche) it seems to me that it is more helpful to use Weber's concept of elective affinity [*Wahlverwandtschaft*] to understand how these two dimensions relate in the culture of liberationist Christianity. I will return to this question below (pp. 68–70). Let me only raise here the hypothesis that this elective affinity is based on a *common matrix of political and religious beliefs*, both being a 'body of individual and collective convictions that are outside the realm of empirical verification and experimentation . . . but which provide significance and coherence to the subjective experience of those who have them'.[7]

Some suggestions by Lucien Goldmann in his book *The Hidden God* may help us to understand this common matrix, which he called 'faith'. As we saw in chapter 1, he used the concept of faith – on the condition of leaving out 'the individual, historical and social contingencies that link it to some specific religion, or even to the positive religions in general' – to define a certain total attitude, common to religions and to social utopias, which refers to *trans-individual values* and is based on a wager.[8]

Goldmann opposed the transcendent religious value (God) and the immanent utopian one (the human community), but in Latin American liberationist Christianity, community is itself one of the most central trans-individual values, possessing both a transcendent and an immanent, an ethical/religious and a social/political, meaning.

This common matrix is an important condition for the development of a process of elective affinity in Latin America between religious ethics and social utopias. The Brazilian sociologist Pedro Ribeiro argues, however, that in the 'liberationist Church' the relationship between religious and political practice is deeper than an elective affinity: 'it has to be understood as a dialectical unity, perceiving religion and politics as two moments of a single reality: the practices of social transformation implemented by the popular classes'.[9] I would add only that the concept of elective affinity can be expanded to include the possibility of achieving a sort of dialectical fusion.

I have been emphasizing the fusion and the unity, but it is important to refer also to the difference and the distance between the two: not being a political movement, liberation theology does not have a programme, nor does it formulate precise economic or political aims. Acknowledging the autonomy of the political sphere, it leaves such issues to the political parties of the Left, limiting itself to social and moral critique against injustice, the raising of popular consciousness, the spreading of utopian hopes, and the promotion of initiatives 'from below'. On the other hand, even when supporting a political movement (e.g. the Sandinista Front), liberation theologians often keep a critical distance, confronting the actual practice of the movement with the emancipatory hopes of the poor.

Liberationist Christianity and liberation theology influence only a minority of the Latin American Churches, in most of which the dominant tendency is rather conservative or moderate. However, their impact is far from being negligible, particularly in Brazil, where the Episcopal Conference (CNBB), despite insistent pressure from the Vatican, has refused to condemn liberation theology. (This may change, since in 1995 a conservative was elected head of the CNBB.) As a matter of fact, the Latin American Church has ceased to appear as a homogeneous corporation. From one country to another one can find not only different but sometimes entirely opposed orientations: for instance, in Argentina, during the military dictatorship and its 'dirty war' (thirty thousand killed or 'disappeared') against 'subversion', the Church condoned, by its obsequious silence, the policy of the regime; now it calls for a 'pardon' of the torturers and killers of the Armed Forces, and mobilizes all its strength against the real danger threatening the nation . . . divorce. Similarly, in Colombia, the Church remains committed body and soul to the oligarchic system, and legitimates in the name of religion the war against atheistic communism. On the other hand, in Brazil, the Church denounced, from 1970 onwards, the military regime, and during the last twenty-five years it has supported the workers' and peasants' struggle for better wages or agrarian reform.

Within the Church in each country, one can also find opposing tendencies – as in Nicaragua, where many priests and members of religious orders supported the Sandinista Revolution, while most bishops sided with the *contras*. One can see a sharp differentiation within continent-wide institutions too: while CELAM, controlled since 1972 by the conservatives, wages an intensive struggle against liberation theology, CLAR, the Conference of Latin American Religious (assembling the religious orders: Jesuits, Dominicans, Franciscans, etc) does not hide its sympathy for the 'Church of the Poor'.

Nevertheless, it would be a very distorted picture to present the Church as divided between revolutionary and counter-revolutionary factions. First of all, many priests, nuns and bishops (as well as lay organizers) are not political at all and react essentially according to moral and religious criteria. Depending on the circumstances, they may be temporarily attracted to one or the other position. Moreover, there is a full rainbow of shades between the two extremes. One can distinguish at least four tendencies within the Latin American Churches:

1. A very small group of fundamentalists, defending ultra-reactionary and sometimes semi-fascist ideas: for instance, the group 'Tradition, Family and Property'.

2. A powerful conservative and traditionalist current, hostile to liberation theology and organically linked to the ruling classes (as well as to the Roman Curia): for instance, the CELAM leadership.

3. A reformist and moderate current (with a certain intellectual autonomy in relation to the Roman authorities), ready to defend human rights and support certain social demands of the poor: this is the position which prevailed at the Puebla Conference in 1979 and (to some extent) at Santo Domingo in 1992.

4. A small but influential minority of radicals, sympathetic to liberation theology and capable of active solidarity with the popular, workers' and peasants' movements. Its best-known representatives have been bishops (or cardinals) such as Mendez Arceo and Samuel Ruiz (Mexico), Pedro Casaldaliga and Paulo Arns (Brazil), Leonidas Proano (Ecuador), Oscar Romero (El Salvador), etc. Within this current, the most advanced section is represented by revolutionary Christians: the 'Christians for Socialism Movement' and other tendencies which identify with Sandinismo, Camilo Torres or Christian Marxism.

This means that the division inside the Church cannot be reduced to the usual vertical model: 'those from below' (popular Christian movements, base communities, Christian trade unionists) against 'those from above' (the hierarchy, bishops and heads of the institution). It is also horizontal, running through the whole clerical body, and dividing into different if not opposed tendencies: the episcopal conferences, the religious orders, the diocesan clergy and the lay movements. But one should not forget that one is dealing with contradictions inside an institution which has carefully preserved its unity, not only because all sides involved want to avoid a schism, but also because its religious aims appear non-reducible to the social or political arena.

Origins and development of liberationist Christianity

What are the reasons for the rise of this new current breaking with a long conservative and regressive tradition? Why was it able to develop in the Latin American Church at a given historical moment?

One of the most significant attempts to explain this phenomenon is the one put forward by Thomas C. Bruneau, a well-known North American specialist on the Brazilian Church: according to him, the Catholic Church began to innovate because it wanted to preserve its influence. Faced with the rise of religious rivals (the Protestant Churches, various sects) and political competition (left-wing movements), a decline in the recruitment of priests, and a financial crisis, the Church elite understood that it had to find a new way, and turned to the lower classes. What was at stake, in the last analysis, was the institutional interests of the Church, broadly understood: 'The Church as institution changed not so much for opportunistic reasons as it did to maintain influence which was itself defined by changing normative orientations.'[10]

This type of analysis is not without value, but it remains basically inadequate. First of all, it rests upon a circular argument: the Church changed because it wanted to keep or broaden its influence, but this influence, in turn, was already being redefined by new normative orientations (towards the dominated classes). The question is: where did these changed orientations originate? Why did the Church no longer conceive its influence in the traditional way – through its relations with the social elites, with political power? The explanation merely shifts the question. Moreover, Bruneau's concept of 'influence', even in its broad meaning (inclusive of the whole spiritual dimension), does not account for the profound ethical-religious upheaval which took place – often in the form of genuine conversions among the social actors (both clergy and lay men and women) who had decided to get involved, sometimes at the risk of their lives, in the new social movement.

Another useful, though still too one-sided, explanation is that put forward by certain sociologists with links to the Christian Left: the Church changed because the people 'took over' the institution, converted it, and made it act in their interests.[11] This probably corresponds to one aspect of reality – especially in the Brazilian case – but once again the question immediately arises: why was it possible for the popular classes to 'convert' the Church to their cause at a given moment? This sort of analysis also tends to under-estimate what Leonardo Boff (elegantly borrowing a Marxist concept) calls 'the *relative autonomy* of the ecclesiastical-religious field'[12] – that is, the cultural and social determinations specific to the Church, without which its 'opening to the people' from the 1960s onwards cannot be understood.

I would like to suggest a third hypothesis to explain the genesis of liberationist Christianity as a social movement in Latin America: namely, that it was the result of a combination or convergence of changes within and without the Church in the late 1950s, and that it developed from the periphery to the centre of the institution.

The internal change affected the Catholic Church as a whole: it was the development since World War II of new theological currents, particularly in Germany (Bultmann, Moltmann, Metz, Rahner) and France (Calvez, Congar, Lubac, Chenu, Duquoc), new forms of social Christianity (the worker priests, Father Lebret's humanist economics), a growing openness to the concerns of modern philosophy and the social sciences. The pontificate of John XXIII (1958–63) and the Vatican II Council (1962–65) legitimated and systematized these new orientations, laying the foundation for a new epoch in the history of the Church.

At the same time, a wrenching social and political change was under way in Latin America: (1) from the 1950s onwards, the industrialization of the continent, under the hegemony of multinational capital, 'developed underdevelopment' – in André Gunder-Frank's now famous formula – that is, fostered greater dependency, deepened social divisions, stimulated rural exodus and urban growth, and concentrated a new working class as well as an immense 'pooretariat'[13] in the larger towns, (2) With the Cuban Revolution of 1959, a new historical period opened in Latin America characterized by the intensification of social struggles, the appearance of guerrilla movements, a succession of military coups and a crisis of legitimacy of the political system.

It was the *convergence* of these very different series of changes which created the conditions of possibility for the emergence of the new 'Church of the Poor', whose origins, it should be noted, date back to *before* Vatican II. In a symbolic way, one might say that the radical Christian current was born in January 1959 at the moment when Fidel Castro, Che Guevara and their comrades marched into Havana, while in Rome John XXIII issued his first call for the convening of the Council.

The new social movement arose first among the groups which were located at the intersection of these two sets of changes: the lay movements (and some members of the clergy) active among student youth and in poor neighbourhoods. In other words, the process of *radicalization* of Latin American Catholic culture which was to lead to the formation of liberationist Christianity did not start, top–down, from the upper reaches of the Church, as the functionalist analyses pointing to the hierarchy's search for influence would suggest, nor from the bottom up, as argued by certain 'popular-orientated' interpretations, but from the periphery to the centre. The categories or social sectors encompassed in the religious-ecclesiastical field that were to become the driving force of renewal were all, in one way or another, marginal or peripheral in relation to the institution: lay movements and their advisers, lay experts, foreign priests, religious orders. The first bishops to be affected were generally those with links to one or another of these categories. In some cases, the movement advanced towards the 'centre' and influenced episcopal conferences (particularly in Brazil); in others, it remained blocked at the 'periphery' of the institution.

Lay Catholic movements, such as Catholic University Youth, Catholic Workers Youth and Catholic Action, or popular educational movements (Brazil), committees for the promotion of land reform (Nicaragua), Federations of Christian Peasants (El Salvador) and above all, the base communities, were, during the early 1960s, the social arena in which Christians actively committed themselves to people's struggles, reinterpreted the Gospel in the light of their practice, and, in some cases, were drawn towards Marxism.

It is no wonder that these movements, 'plunged' directly into a society in crisis, were most permeable to the social, political and cultural currents of their environment. Several of them began to undergo a dynamic of autonomization, similar to that of the French JEC (Catholic Student Youth) analysed by Danièle Hervieu-Léger: in the first stage, the Christian activists 'assumed fully' the milieu which they intended to win over to the word of God by intensely identifying with its collective aspirations; then came the demand for autonomy, in so far as these profane commitments did not fit in with religious norms; finally, the conflict with the hierarchy exploded when the movement publicly adopted a stand different from the official position of the Church on one or another social or political issue.[14] This was exactly what happened in the Brazilian JUC in the early 1960s and, as a result of their conflict with the Church, the main leaders and activists of the Christian student movement decided to form a new political organization, of Marxist inspiration, Popular Action (1962). In Chile too, something similar happened, with the result that leaders of the JUC and Christian Democratic Youth formed the United People's Action Movement (MAPU), a Marxist party, in 1969.

Another group of lay people who played a key role in the formation of liberationist Christianity – although they did not go through the same dynamic of autonomization – were the teams of experts who worked for the bishops and episcopal conferences, preparing briefings and proposing pastoral plans, and sometimes drafting their statements. These economists, sociologists, urban planners, theologians and lawyers constituted a kind of lay intellectual apparatus of the Church, which introduced into the institution the latest developments in the social sciences – which, in Latin America from the 1960s onwards, meant Marxist sociology and economics (dependency theory). The influence of these teams was decisive in formulating certain documents of the Brazilian Episcopate, in preparing the Medellín Conference (1968), and so on.

Within the institution itself, the religious orders were in the vanguard of the new practice and of the new theological thinking. This was true in particular of the Jesuits, Dominicans, Franciscans, Maryknolls, Capuchins and female orders. The religious orders – a total of 157,000 people in all Latin America, mostly women – are the single largest group staffing the new social pastorals and creating base communities. Most well-known liberation theologians are religious and, as mentioned earlier, the CLAR (founded in 1959) used to take far more radical positions than the CELAM. In some countries, such as Nicaragua, this difference is reflected in a more or less open conflict between the bishops and the religious orders, while elsewhere (Brazil), the episcopal conference supported the progressive orders.

How can we explain the particularly prominent commitment of the orders? One element that must be considered is the protest – both against the world and against the Church – involved in the very nature of the monastic utopia itself; in an article written in 1971, the French sociologist Jean Séguy suggests that this utopian dimension can help us to understand 'certain links between Catholic religious orders and revolutionary activity' in Latin America.[15] Moreover, religious orders enjoy a certain autonomy within the Church, and are less subject to the direct control of the episcopal hierarchy than the diocesan clergy. Another important factor is the high level of education received by the religious, their familiarity with modern thought and the social sciences, their direct contact with contemporary theology as taught in Louvain, Paris and Germany. Certain orders, such as the Jesuits and Dominicans, are genuine networks of 'organic' intellectuals of the Church, engaged in a constant exchange and dialogue with the academic and 'profane' intellectual world – a world which, in Latin America, is substantially influenced by Marxism.

The last 'peripheric' group which decisively contributed to the upsurge of liberationist Christianity is that of the foreign priests and religious, notably from Spain, France and North America. For instance, half of the eighty priests in Chile who published a statement in April 1971 endorsing the transition to socialism were foreigners; similar phenomena can be found in Central America. One possible explanation is selective self-recruitment: the priests and religious available for missions to Latin American countries probably represent a sector of the Church that is particularly sensitive to problems of poverty and the Third World. Many of the French missionaries had participated in, or had first-hand knowledge of, the experience of the worker priests, and among the 'Spaniards' there was a high percentage of Basques, coming from a region where the Church has a tradition of resisting the government. An additional reason is the fact that foreign clergy members were often sent by the bishops to the most remote and poorest regions, or to the new shantytowns which have proliferated in the large urban areas of the continent – that is, wherever traditional dioceses did not exist. The contrast between the living conditions in their country of origin and the stark poverty they discovered in Latin America caused among many of them a genuine moral and religious conversion to the liberation movement of the poor. As noted by Brian H. Smith, an American sociologist, in his important work on the Church in Chile, the foreign priests, who were initially inspired only by the same reforming concerns as the bishops, 'had become radicalized by what they had seen and experienced in working-class areas', and therefore 'moved decidedly to the Left in both their theological opinions and their social analysis'.[16]

Nor was the radicalization process that emerged among certain Christian (clerical and/or lay) circles in the 1960s limited to Brazil and Chile; under various forms, analogous developments occurred in other countries too: the best-known case is, of course, that of Camilo Torres, a priest who organized a militant popular movement and then joined the National Liberation Army (ELN), a Castroist guerrilla movement in Colombia, in 1965. Camilo Torres was killed in 1966 in a clash with the Army but his martyrdom had a deep emotional and political impact on Latin American Christians, leading to the rise of a significant current that identified with his legacy. Moreover, groups of radicalized priests organized just about everywhere – Priests for the Third World (Sacerdotes para el Tercer Mundo) in Argentina in 1966, the National Organization for Social Integration (ONIS) in Peru in 1968, the Golconda group in Colombia, also in 1968 – while a growing number of Christians became actively involved in popular struggles. They reinterpreted the Gospel in the light of this practice and, sometimes, discovered in Marxism a key to the understanding of social reality, as well as a guide to changing it.

This explosion of activity, coming in the context of renewal that followed the Vatican II Council, finally began to shake the whole Church of the continent. When the bishops met at the Latin American Episcopal Conference in Medellín, in 1968, new resolutions were adopted which, for the first time, not only denounced existing structures as based on injustice, the violation of the fundamental rights of the people and 'institutionalized violence', but also asserted the Church's solidarity with the people's aspiration to 'liberation from all servitude'. They even acknowledged that, in certain circumstances – such as the existence of a prolonged tyranny, of either a personal or a structural character – revolutionary insurrection was legitimate.

Similar phenomena occurred in other regions of the Third World (the Philippines, for example) and, on a smaller scale, even in Europe and the United States. Its greater success in Latin America results, in part, from the fact that it is the Catholic continent *par excellence*, where the great majority of the population is immersed from birth in Roman Catholic religious culture. At the same time, Latin America is, so to speak, 'the weakest link in the Catholic chain': in a context of increasing economic dependency and growing poverty, the victory of the Cuban revolution started a wave of social struggles and revolutionary attempts throughout the continent which has not ceased from 1960 to this day. These were the social and historical conditions in which a significant sector of the Church actively embraced the cause of the poor and their self-emancipation.

Vatican II Council undoubtedly contributed to this evolution, but one should not forget that the first signs of radicalization (particularly in Brazil) unfolded well before the Council. Furthermore, Vatican II resolutions failed go beyond the bounds of a modernization, an *aggiornamento*, an opening to the world. It is true that this opening undermined ancient dogmatic certainties and made Catholic culture permeable to new ideas and 'external' influences. In opening itself to the modern world, the Church, particularly in Latin America, could not escape the social conflicts which were shaking the world, nor the influence of various philosophical and political currents – especially Marxism, which was at that time (the 1960s) the dominant cultural tendency among the continent's intelligentsia.

It is in this specific context that liberation theology was born. The most advanced Latin American theologians, dissatisfied with the 'development theology' which was dominant in the Latin American Churches, began to raise the theme of liberation as early as the late 1960s. Hugo Assmann, a Brazilian theologian trained in Frankfurt, played a pioneering role in elaborating the first elements of a Christian and liberationist critique of *desarrollismo* (developmentalism) in 1970.[17]

But it was in 1974, with the publication of *Liberation Theology – Perspectives*, by Gustavo Gutiérrez, a Peruvian Jesuit and former student at the Catholic universities of Louvain and Lyon, that liberation theology was truly born. Of course, this work was not born *ex-nihilo*: it was the expression of ten years of praxis by socially committed Christians and several years of discussions among progressive Latin American theologians.[18]

In his book, Gutiérrez advanced certain highly original and unconventional ideas that had a profound impact on Latin American Catholic culture. First of all, he emphasized the need to break with the dualism inherited from Greek thought: there are not two realities as alleged, the one 'temporal', the other 'spiritual', nor are there two histories, the one 'sacred', the other 'profane'. There is only one history, and it is in this human and temporal history that Redemption and the Kingdom of God must be realized. The point is not to wait passively for salvation from above: the biblical Exodus shows us 'the construction of the human being by himself through the historical political struggle'. Exodus is therefore the model for a salvation that is not individual and private but communitarian and public, in which it is not the soul of one individual as such that is at stake, but the redemption and liberation of a whole enslaved people. In this perspective, the poor are no longer an object of pity or charity but, like the Hebrew slaves, the agents of their own emancipation.

What does this mean for Latin America? According to Gutiérrez, the poor people of the continent are 'in exile in their own land', but at the same time 'on an Exodus march towards their redemption'. Rejecting the ideology of development which has 'become synonymous with reformism and modernization' – that is, with limited, timid, ineffective measures that only make dependency worse – he believed that 'only a radical destruction of the present state of things, a profound transformation of the ownership system, the coming to power of the exploited class, a social revolution will put an end to this dependency. They alone will allow a transition to a socialist society, or at least will make it possible.'[19] In a similar vein, the Chilean Jesuit Gonzalo Arroyo rejected the Western theories that defined development as 'the passage between two ideal types of society, the "traditional" and the "modern", without reference to the concrete situations of power, and implicitly identifying the modern type with the industrial capitalist society'.[20]

Interestingly enough, this is a far more radical position than the one advocated at that time by the dominant currents of the Latin American Left (the Communist Parties and left-nationalist movements), which did not challenge capitalism nor consider the transition to socialism a contemporary revolutionary task in Latin America: they called instead for a 'national-democratic transformation'.

Shortly thereafter, in April 1972, the first continent-wide gathering of the Christians for Socialism movement – inspired by two Chilean Jesuits, the theologian Pablo Richard and the economist Gonzalo Arroyo, and supported by the Mexican bishop Sergio Mendez Arceo – was held in Santiago de Chile. This ecumenical movement, composed of Catholics as well as Protestants, represented the most radical form of liberation theology, going as far as attempting a synthesis between Marxism and Christianity – for which the Chilean episcopate soon rewarded it with a ban. The final resolution of the 1972 meeting proclaimed the participants' support, as Christians, of the struggle for socialism in Latin America. One of the sections of this historic document explains the dialectic of faith and revolution in the following terms:

> The real-life presence of the faith in the very heart of revolutionary praxis provides for a fruitful interaction. The Christian faith becomes a critical and dynamic leaven for revolution. Faith intensifies the demand that the class struggle move decisively towards the liberation of all men – in particular, those who suffer the most acute forms of oppression. It also stresses our orientation towards a total transformation of society rather than merely a transformation of economic structures. Thus, in and through committed Christians, faith makes its own contribution to the construction of a society that is qualitatively distinct from the present one, and to the appearance of the New Man.
>
> But revolutionary commitment also has a critical and motivating function vis-à-vis the Christian faith. It criticizes the open and the more subtle forms of complicity between the faith and the dominant culture during the course of history. . . . Christians involved in the process of liberation vividly come to realize that the demands of revolutionary praxis . . . force them to rediscover the central themes of the gospel message – only now they are freed from their ideological dress.
>
> The real context for a living faith today is the history of oppression and of the struggle for liberation from this oppression. To situate oneself within this context, however, one must truly participate in the process of liberation by joining parties and organizations that are authentic instruments of the struggle of the working class.[21]

At the Conference of Latin American Bishops held in Puebla in 1979, a real attempt to bring things back under control took place: CELAM, the organizing body of the conference, forbade liberation theologians to attend the conference. They were nevertheless present in the city of Puebla and, through the mediation of certain bishops, exercised a real influence on the debates. The ensuing compromise was summarized by the now famous formula of 'the Church's preferential option for the poor' – a sufficiently general phrase to allow each current to interpret it according to its own inclinations.

In an attempt to answer the challenge, Rome issued in 1984 an *Instruction on Some Aspects of 'Liberation Theology'* signed by the Sacred Congregation for the Doctrine of the Faith (led by Cardinal Ratzinger), denouncing liberation theology as a new type of heresy based on the use of Marxist concepts. The reactions of Latin American theologians and important sectors of the Church – particularly in Brazil – forced the Vatican to backtrack somewhat. In 1985, a new (apparently) more positive instruction was issued, *Christian Liberty and Liberation*, which retrieved certain themes of liberation theology, but 'spiritualized' them and stripped them of their social revolutionary content. At around the same time, the Pope sent a letter to the Brazilian Church assuring it of his support and recognizing the legitimacy of liberation theology.

The debate around the two Roman instructions was unacceptable for the Vatican, used to the traditional rule *Roma locuta, causa finita*. From that moment on, the confrontation with liberation theology has continued not in the field of theological discussion but in that of episcopal power: through the systematic appointment of conservative bishops (to replace those who die or retire). Rome's aim is to marginalize the radical currents and reassert its control over episcopal conferences deemed to have gone too far – chief among which is the Brazilian CNBB. The recent change of majority among the Brazilian bishops, with the victory of the conservatives, seems to indicate substantial successes for the Vatican's strategy. We shall return to this issue in the concluding chapter.

As far as the Church as an institutional structure is concerned, the big change since the 1960s has been the rise of the *ecclesiastic base communities* (Comunidades Eclesiales de Base – CEBs), particularly in Brazil, where they encompass hundreds of thousands (perhaps millions) of Christians, and, on a lesser scale, throughout the continent. The base community is a small group of neighbours who belong to the same popular quarter, shantytown, village or rural zone, and meet regularly to pray, sing, celebrate, read the Bible and discuss it in the light of their own life experience. It should be stressed that CEBs are much more conventionally religious than is commonly realized: they value and practise a number of traditional prayers and rites (rosaries, nocturnal vigils, adorations and celebrations like processions and pilgrimages) which belong to popular religion.[22]

In the urban areas CEBs are overwhelmingly women's organizations – in São Paulo (Brazil) for instance, according to recent studies women comprise more than 60 per cent of participants. Thanks to this participation, many women are able to 'enter into the realm of politics on the basis of their class position and gender interests within that class'.[23] The feminization of the movement is reinforced by the fact that most of the pastoral agents that help to organize CEBs in the popular urban areas are women from the (feminine) religious orders.

The CEBs are part of a diocese and have more or less regular links with pastoral agents: priests, religious brothers and, more often, sisters. They do not organize the majority of the believers, but only what the Brazilian sociologist Pedro Ribeiro calls 'the popular religious elite', an active and practising group of believers who belong to the poor layers; the traditional parish continues to respond to the religious needs of the non-practising majority and to the middle-class or rich churchgoers.[24] Little by little the discussions and activities of the community broaden, generally with the assistance of the clergy, and begin to include social tasks: struggles for housing, electricity, sewerage or water in the urban *barrios*, struggles for land in the countryside. They contribute notably to the creation and growth of such social movements as (in the Brazilian case) the Movement against the High Cost of Living, the Movement against Unemployment, the Movement for Public Transportation, the Landless Peasant Movement, and many others.[25] In certain cases, the experience of these struggles leads to politicization and to several leaders or members of the CEBs joining workers' parties or revolutionary fronts.

As Daniel Levine points out, one can better understand this dynamic by referring to Weber's remarks about the congregational [*Gemeinde*] religion:

> One way to appreciate the significance of what CEBs may represent is to note the way in which they create and nurture a space for the practice of congregational religion within contemporary Catholicism. . . . The promotion of justice itself is rooted in the core of religious faith. . . . When these ideas are placed in the context of solidarity, reinforcing group structures, the results can be explosive. . . . Weber's summary comment suggests the way in which changes in religion and politics converge with revolutionary implications. 'The more religion became congregational,' he wrote, 'the more did political circumstances contribute to the transfiguration of the ethics of the subjugated.'

Weber's mistake was to ignore the possibility that such a development could take place in a Catholic context.[26]

There are also, as the Brazilian sociologist Yvo Lesbaupin emphasized, many aspects of the CEBs that correspond to the ideal-type of sect according to Troeltsch (or Weber): the participation of lay people, the importance attributed to the Bible, the communitarian life, fraternity and mutual help, and above all 'the elective affinity with democratic structures' (Weber). But at the same time the base community is not a 'sect' because it is part of the Catholic Church and intimately linked to its clergy.[27]

The CEB experience, because of its powerful democratic component, has often contributed a new quality to the social and political movements which it has nurtured: rooted in the daily life of the populace and in their humble and concrete concerns, it has encouraged grass-roots self-organization, and a distrust of political manipulation, electoral rhetoric and state paternalism.

This has also sometimes included a negative counterpart: the so called *basismo* ('basism') leading to a rejection of theory and to hostility towards political organization. The debate on these questions has been carried on among the theologians themselves, some displaying a more 'populist', others a more 'political' sensitivity; the dominant tendency being the search for a practice that transcends one-sided methods. In an article from 1982, Frei Betto criticized both elitist and populist attitudes:

> In the practice of the popular pastoral, one has to avoid two deviations: ecclesiastic populism and ecclesiastic vanguardism. Ecclesiastic populism is the attitude of pastoral agents who think of the people as if they were sacred, as if they had a pure consciousness, untouched by dominant ideology. . . . On the other side, ecclesiastic vanguardism is the attitude of pastoral agents who consider the people incapable and ignorant, and consider themselves self-sufficient in the orientation of the popular pastoral. This tendency believes that it has nothing to learn from the people.[28]

At any rate, several of the major struggles for democracy and social emancipation in Latin America in the last twenty-five years have only been possible thanks to the contribution of the CEBs and liberationist Christianity. This is the case, in particular, in Brazil and Central America: whatever the consequences of the present 'normalization' policy applied by Rome to the Latin American Catholic Church may be – and one cannot rule out a substantial victory of the Vatican's strategy and the subsequent weakening of liberationist Christianity – certain historical changes have already taken place: the formation of the Workers' Party in Brazil, the Sandinista Revolution in Nicaragua, and the popular insurgency in El Salvador. Later we shall look at each of these three experiences more closely.

Modernity and the Critique of Modernity in Liberation Theology

How does liberation theology – and the social movement it inspires – relate to modernity? This section relates mainly to Catholic liberation theology, which has some particular aspects distinct from its Protestant counterpart.

The antinomy between tradition and modernity is often used in the social sciences – particularly in relation to Third World countries – as the main key for the interpretation of economic, social, political and cultural reality. The usefulness of these categories is undeniable but one has to avoid the risk of reducing all social analysis to a dualist dichotomy, unable to account for the deeply ambivalent – or polyvalent – character of such phenomena. Far from being always contradictory, modernity and tradition are often articulated, associated and combined in a complementary way – a process in which the traditional components are not necessarily a dead weight ('relics of the past') but active constituents of cultural renewal. One should not forget, moreover, that modernity itself is an ambiguous phenomenon, shot through with tensions between the heritages of the Industrial Revolution and of the French Revolution, between liberalism and democracy, between instrumental and substantive rationality.

Certain European authors insist that there is an irreducible internal contradiction in liberation theology between its modern dimension and its critique of modernity. My hypothesis is that the originality of liberation theology results precisely from a synthesis that supersedes (some would say 'dialectically') the classic opposition between tradition and modernity. Liberation theology and liberationist Christianity are, at the same time, at the most advanced point of the modernist current inside the Catholic Church, and inheritors of the Catholic traditional – or *intransigent*, to use Émile Poulat's terminology – mistrust of modernity. Let us briefly examine these two aspects.

Modernity of liberation theology

Defence of modern liberties

Liberation theology fully assimilates the modern values of the French Revolution: liberty, equality, fraternity, democracy and the separation between Church and State. As Leonardo Boff emphasizes, the new Latin American theology does not feel any kinship with a certain tradition of the institutional Church, which, 'since the sixteenth century, defined itself by being "against": against the Reformation (1521), against the Revolutions (1789), against values which are today generally accepted, like freedom of consciousness, but were still condemned in 1856 by Gregorius XVI as *deliramentum*, freedom of opinion, damned as anathema and "pestilential error" by the same Pope, against democracy, etc'. In a similar vein, Gustavo Gutiérrez categorically rejects the regressive position of the nineteenth-century Popes, which allowed the most conservative sectors of the Church (those that nourished the hope of a restoration of the ancient social order) to eliminate or reduce to silence, with strong condemnations, 'the groups which were the most open to the movements for modern liberties and to critical thought'. For this reason, he celebrates Vatican II as a salutary awakening to modern society, to the great demands of modernity (human rights, liberties, social equality) – in short, as 'a gust of fresh air in a stifling room'.[29]

This modernist option led some liberation theologians to a critique of the authoritarianism and the limitations on freedom of expression inside the Church itself. If all of them share a democratic ecclesiology, which downplays clerical power and conceives the Church as 'the people of God', built from the grass roots up, few have gone so far as Leonardo Boff in the explicit challenge to Roman power. In his book *Church, Charisma and Power* (1981) he criticizes, in a quite direct way, the hierarchical authority inside the Church, its Roman-imperial and feudal style of power, its tradition of intolerance and dogmatism (symbolized during many centuries by the Inquisition), its repression of all criticism coming from below, and its refusal to accept freedom of thought. He also denounces the Church's pretention to infallibility and the excessive personal power of the Popes (comparable to those of the General Secretary of the Soviet Communist Party!). As is known, Leonardo Boff was condemned by Rome, after the publication of this book, to a year of 'obsequious silence'. . . .[30]

Since the Protestant Reformation, there has hardly been a stronger challenge (from inside) to the Church's structure of power and authority. But Boff's approach is far from being shared by all liberation theologians. Gustavo Gutiérrez, for instance, emphasized already in 1971: 'To focus on intra-ecclesiastical problems – as often happens with certain forms of protest inside the Church, especially in the developed countries – is to miss the richest possibility for a true renewal of the Church.' In his view, which is shared by many other progressive Catholics, it is through active commitment to the outside world that the internal changes will take place.[31]

There is one sensitive area in relation to modern freedoms where liberation theologians are most cautious, and where the otherwise open-minded bishops and clergy can be quite conservative: sexual ethics, divorce, contraception and abortion – in short, women's free disposition over their own bodies. Is the theologians' silence purely tactical (to avoid conflicts with the hierarchy), or does it result from pre-modern convictions, produced by a traditional education inspired by the philosophy of natural law? In any case, this is one of the issues where the gap between lay people and clergy, even within liberationist Christianity, is most evident.

It is a fact that on questions involving the family and sexuality, the interruption of pregnancy and birth control, even as progressive a Church as the Brazilian still defends traditionalist and backward positions – quite close to those preached by the Pope – which are far from being shared by all lay Catholics. Most of the progressive Catholic activists – but only the most advanced liberation theologians such as Frei Betto – accept that abortion should be decriminalized. Need I emphasize that this is a matter of life or death for millions of Latin American women, who are still compelled to have illegal abortions with tragic consequences?

Nevertheless, some liberation theologians have begun to reflect on the question of the specific oppression of women. Their current thinking, still tentative, is reflected in the collection of interviews about this issue (with Gustavo Gutiérrez, Leonardo Boff, Frei Betto, Pablo Richard, Hugo Assmann and others) published by Elsa Tamez in 1986.[32]

More importantly, Christian women themselves are beginning to speak out, and the voices of women theologians, religious and lay activists such as Elsa Tamez, Yvone Gebara, Maria José Rosario Nunes and Maria Clara Bingemer are being heard, raising the question of the double oppression of Latin American women, and the multiple forms of discrimination they suffer in society as a whole and in the Church itself.

The positive evaluation of the social sciences and their integration into theology

For a long time the use of the social sciences by theology was rejected by the Catholic Church as a 'modernist' heresy. This began to change after World War II and, finally, during the Vatican II Council, a recommendation was made to use the discoveries made by the *scientiarum profanum, imprimis psychologiae et sociologiae* (in *Gaudium et Spes*). However, in Latin America, and especially in Brazil, under the influence of Father Lebret and his Centres of Humanist Economy, social sciences had been quite systematically used since the 1950s, well before the Council. As we saw above, after 1960, Marxist social science – political economy as well as the class analysis – and especially its Latin American variants such as dependency theory, became the main 'socio-analytical' instrument of progressive Christians. It was considered by liberation theologians an indispensable 'tool' to understand and judge social reality – particularly in order to explain the causes of poverty in Latin America – and therefore as a necessary mediation between theological reflection and pastoral practice.

It should be specified that for this eminently modern theological conception the aim is not at all to submit social sciences to religious imperatives, nor to make them into a new *ancilla theologiae* (according to the scholastic definition of philosophy as 'theology's handmaid'). Liberation theology acknowledges the complete independence of scientific research from the presuppositions or dogmas of religion, and limits itself to the use of its results to nourish its own work. As Gutiérrez writes: 'the use of social sciences in order to better know social reality requires a great respect for their own field of action and for the legitimate autonomy of politics'.[33] At the same time, it is evident that social, ethical and religious criteria determine, to a large extent, what type of social science will be chosen by the theologians, and which scientific method will be privileged by them.

The critique of modernity in liberation theology

While liberation theology claims for itself the heritage of the French Revolution and its main political values in terms of human rights and democracy, it takes a much more critical stance in relation to another aspect of modernity – the industrial/capitalist civilization, as it has 'really existed' from the eighteenth century until today. One can define the modern bourgeois/industrial world as a civilization based on technical and scientific progress, accumulation of capital, expansion of the production and consumption of commodities, individualism, reification [*Versachlichung*], the spirit of economic calculation [*Rechenhaftigkeit*], instrumental rationality [*Zweckrationalität*] and disenchantment of the world [*Entzauberung der Welt*] – to use some of Max Weber's well-known formulations.

The last 'error' mentioned in the long list of Pius X's *Syllabus* (1864) is the heresy according to which 'the Roman Pontif can and should reconcile himself and compromise with progress, liberalism and modern civilization'. Without by any means sharing this stance of global rejection, liberation theology nevertheless criticizes, in a most uncompromising way, the harmful and evil consequences of a certain kind of economic progress, liberalism and modern civilization for the poor in Latin America. This criticism combines traditional elements – that is, the reference to pre-modern social, ethical and religious values – and values of modernity itself.

The critique of capitalism

Liberation theology inherited from the Church the tradition of Catholic hostility or 'aversion' (Weber's term: *Abneigung*) towards the spirit of capitalism. However, it has considerably modified and modernized it: (a) by radicalizing it in a much more general and systematic way; (b) by combining the moral criticism with a modern (mainly Marxist) critique of exploitation; (c) by replacing charity with social justice; (d) by refusing to idealize the patriarchal past; and (e) by proposing as an alternative a socialized economy.

Nevertheless, without referring to this tradition one cannot understand the intransigent nature of liberation theology's anti-capitalism, and its powerful ethical/religious thrust.

The irreconcilable (Weber's term: *Unversöhnlich*) opposition or 'principled struggle' [*prinzipiellen Kampf*] of Catholic ethics against capitalist modernity inspires the criticism by liberation theologians of the reconciliation between the Church and the modern (bourgeois) world. According to the Chilean theologian Pablo Richard, one of the founders of the 'Christians for Socialism' movement:

for the oppressed classes, this convergence or coherence between faith and modern world is an alien reality, because it represents the sanctification of oppression. The encounter between faith and modern scientific reason, between salvation and human progress, appears therefore as the coherent reflection of the encounter or reconciliation between the Church and the ruling classes. The process of modernization of the Church, and of compromise with the modern world, perverts itself in so far as it legitimizes the system of domination.

He adds the following argument, which seems directly to echo Weber's remarks on the reasons for the 'negative affinity' between the Church and capitalism: 'Christianity, reduced by modernization to a formal code of values and principles, cannot at all interfere with economic calculations, with the law of maximization of profits, with the law of the market'. Economic life follows its course, according to the 'pitiless logic of the economic and political rationality of the modern capitalist system'.[34]

Another characteristic topic of liberation theology is its attack on capitalism as a *false religion*, a new form of idolatry: the idolatry of Money (the ancient god Mammon), of Capital, or of the Market. Combining the (modern) Marxist analysis of commodity fetishism with the (traditional) Old Testamentarian prophetic denunciation of false gods, the Latin American theologians insist on the evil nature of these new, cruel and human-sacrificing idols ('the foreign debt', for example): the capitalist idols or fetishes (in the Marxian meaning) are Molochs that devour human life – an image also used by Marx in *Capital*. The struggle of liberationist Christianity against (capitalist) idolatry is presented as a *war of gods* – as we know, a Weberian concept – between the God of Life and the idols of death (Jon Sobrino), or between the God of Jesus Christ and the multiplicity of gods on the Olympus of the capitalist system (Pablo Richard). Most active in this respect have been the theologians from the DEI (Ecumenical Department of Research, Costa Rica), which in 1980 issued a collection of articles under the significant title *The Struggle of Gods. The Idols of Oppression and the Search for the Liberating God*.[35] This topic has also been central in the writings of a new generation of theologians, such as the brilliant Korean/Brazilian author Jung Mo Sung, who in his writings attacks the 'economic religion' of capitalism and its sacrificial fetishism.[36]

Two of the founders of DEI, Hugo Assmann and Franz Hinkelammert, published in 1989 *The Idolatry of the Market*, a remarkable essay on economics and theology. According to Hinkelammert, in the theology of total market – a combination of economic neo-liberalism and Christian fundamentalism – 'God is nothing more than the transcendentalized personification of market laws. . . . The divinization of the market creates a money-God: *in God we trust*.' Assmann draws attention to the explicit theological content of economic liberalism – Adam Smith's 'hidden hand' as the equivalent of divine providence – and to the cruel sacrificial theology of capitalism, from Malthus to our own day.[37]

Perhaps the greatest novelty of liberation theology in relation to the Church's tradition, however, is that it goes well beyond a moral critique of capitalism, by calling for its abolition. For instance, according to Gutiérrez, the poor need a revolutionary struggle that is able to call

> the existing social order into question from the roots up. It insists that the people must come to power if society is to be truly free and egalitarian. In such a society private ownership of the means of production will be eliminated because it enables a few to expropriate the fruits of labour performed by the many, generates class divisions in society and permits one class to be exploited by another.[38]

Against the privatization of faith

Commenting on Émile Poulat's works on the Catholic tradition, Danièle Hervieu-Léger observes that from the same 'intransigent' background or trunk emerge such different branches as fundamentalism on one side and revolutionary Christianity on the other, their common trait being the rejection of liberalism.[39] It is a fact that liberation theology shares with the most 'intransigent' Catholic tradition the rejection of the privatization of faith and of the – typically modern and liberal – separation of spheres between the religious and the political.

Criticizing the liberal theologies, Gustavo Gutiérrez wrote: 'By focusing their attention on the demands of the bourgeois societies, these theologies accepted the place in which the societies enclosed them: the sphere of private consciousness.'[40] In so far as their viewpoint effectively requires a 're-politicization' of the religious field and a religious intervention in the political field, liberationist Christians will be accused by certain liberal critics of being an obstacle to modernization. For instance, the US functionalist sociologist Ivan Vallier accused the revolutionary priests of exerting a 'regressive and traditionalist' influence in Latin America. Since modernization requires a differentiation of areas 'that allows the non-religious spheres of society to move ahead autonomously, i.e. within nonreligious normative frameworks', the 'clerical radicalism' of the revolutionary priests constitutes an

> implicit refusal to acknowledge that civil and ecclesiastic spheres should be differentiated. By collapsing, at least symbolically, the religious and political levels of society, it not only carries a traditionalizing effect, but it also breeds retrogressive ones, in that political differences are reinforced by religious meanings and identities, which are likely to produce irreconcilable cleavages.

In conclusion, 'clerical radicalism' is negative, because it obstructs 'civic development and processes of nation-building'.[41]

This heavily biased analysis is widely off the mark, but it is true that liberationist Christianity refuses to limit itself to the 'ecclesiastic sphere', leaving the economy and politics to their 'autonomous' development – and from this standpoint one can trace a parallel with the intransigent tradition and its refusal of the modern separation of spheres. As Juan Carlos Scannone emphasizes, liberation theology does not accept the autonomy of the temporal world defended by modern rationalism, or the tranquillizing separation of the spheres (temporal and spiritual) characteristic of the liberal ideology of progress.[42]

However, the kind of analysis represented by Vallier is too superficial and formalist because it does not take into account the fact that Latin American liberationist Christianity does also radically innovate in relation to the tradition: (a) by proposing total separation between the Church and the State; (b) by rejecting the idea of a Christian party or union, and acknowledging the necessary autonomy of social and political movements; (c) by rejecting any idea of a return to a pre-critical 'political Catholicism', and its illusion of a 'new Christendom'; and (d) by favouring Christian participation in secular popular movements or parties.[43]

For liberation theology there is no contradiction between this requirement of modern and secular democracy and the Christian's commitment in the political field. There are two different levels of approach to the relationship between the religious and the political: at the *institutional* level, separation and autonomy must prevail; but on the *ethical/political* level, it is commitment that becomes the essential imperative.

The critique of individualism

According to Gustavo Gutiérrez, 'individualism is the most important note of modern ideology and of bourgeois society. According
to modern mentality, the individual human being is the absolute
beginning, the autonomous centre of decision. Individual initiative
and individual interests are the starting point and the motor of
economic activity'. Most appropriately, he refers in this context to
the writings of Lucien Goldmann, which highlight the opposition
between religion, as a system of trans-individual values, and
the strictly individualistic method of the Enlightenment and the
market economy.[44]

For the liberation theologians and pastoral agents working
with base communities, one of the most negative aspects of urban/
industrial modernity in Latin America – from the social and ethical
viewpoint – is the destruction of the traditional communitarian
links: whole populations are uprooted from their traditional rural
communitarian setting by the development of agro-capitalism
('human beings replaced by sheep' according to Thomas More's
complaint – or rather, in many Latin American countries, by cattle)
and dumped at the periphery of the big urban centres, where they
find a climate of egoistic individualism, unchecked competition
and brutal fight for survival. In a recent book on ecclesiastic base
communities, the Brazilian Jesuit theologian Marcello Azevedo
denounces capitalist modernity as being responsible for the breaking up of all links between the individual and his group, and
presents CEBs as the concentrated expression of the double attempt
at a revival of community, in society and in the Church.[45]

One of the main activities of popular pastorals, like the land
pastoral or the indigenous pastoral, is the defence of traditional
communities (of poor peasants or Indian tribes) threatened by the
voracity of big agro-industrial business or by the great modernizing
projects of the State. In the chaotic periphery of the urban centres,
it aims to rebuild, through the CEBs, a communitarian lifestyle,
with the help of traditions from the rural past still present in the collective memory of the poor – habits of neighbourhood, solidarity
and mutual help. A keen observer of base communities, the North
American theologian and sociologist Harvey Cox, suggests that
through the CEBs the poor population 'is reappropriating a cluster
of stories and a moral tradition that have survived the onslaught
of capitalist modernization and are now beginning to provide an

alternative to the officially established system of values and meanings'. The new Latin American theologies have 'organizational styles [that] stress community against individualism, organic instead of mechanistic modes of living together'.[46]

Are we thérefore confronted with an attempt to return to the pre-modern, traditional organic community – the *Gemeinschaft* described by Tönnies? Yes and no. Yes, in so far as, confronted with a modern society that has, according to Leonardo Boff, 'generated an atomization of existence and a general anonymity of all persons', it tries to create (or recreate) 'communities where people know and recognize each other', ideally characterized by 'direct relations, reciprocity, deep fraternity, mutual help, communion in evangelical ideas and equality among its members'.[47] No, in so far as the communities are not just the reproduction of pre-modern social relationships.

In this area, too, liberationist Christianity will innovate: as Harvey Cox insightfully observes, ecclesiastic base communities contain a typically modern aspect – individual choice, which generates new forms of solidarity that do not have much in common with the archaic rural structures.[48] Their aim is not to reconstruct traditional communities (that is, closed and authoritarian structures), with a system of norms and obligations imposed by family, tribe, locality or religious denomination on each individual from birth. Rather, it is to form a new sort of community that necessarily incorporates some of the most important 'modern liberties' – beginning with the free decision to join or not. By virtue of this modern aspect, one can consider the CEBs as *voluntary utopian groupings*, in the meaning given to this expression by Jean Séguy, that is, groupings whose members participate by their own will, and whose aim (implicit or explicit) is to transform – in a way that is at least optionally radical – the existing global social systems.[49] What the CEBs try to rescue from the communitarian traditions are the 'primary' personal relations, the practice of mutual help, and the sharing of a common faith.

The challenge to economic modernization, the cult of technical progress and the ideology of development

The stance of the Latin American Church in relation to economic development and modern technology before the rise of the CEBs was far from negative. In the framework of what one could call a 'theology of development' – dominant in the years from 1955 to 1960 – it was favourably disposed towards economic modernization, while hoping to correct some of its negative aspects according to the principles of Christian ethics.

With the radicalization of Catholic Action (JUC, JOC, etc) during the 1960s and the rise of liberation theology after the 1970s, this 'developmentist' viewpoint was superseded (in the most advanced sectors of the Church) by a much more critical attitude towards the capitalist model of development, inspired at least in part by Latin American Marxism and dependency theory (for instance, the attacks of someone like André Gunder Frank on the US doctrines of modernization). This new perspective directly influences the social/religious culture of liberationist Christianity, generating the strong belief that the way out for Latin American countries lies not so much in technological modernization as in social change.

For liberation theology, industrial development, the new techniques and the modernization of production, far from being solutions to the social problems of the continent – poverty, social inequality, illiteracy, unemployment, rural migration, urban violence, epidemics, infant mortality – often aggravate and intensify them. According to Hugo Assmann, in a pioneering text written in 1970, 'the excessive price paid for "development" is the growing alienation of large sectors of the community and the repression of all forms of protest'; in his opinion, the great merit of the documents issued by the bishops' conference of Medellín (1968) – even if they are more descriptive than dialectical and structural – is the critical attitude towards 'developmentism'. Gutiérrez too calls into question, in his book from 1974, the ideology of economic development: 'The *desarrollista* option of modernization obscured both the complexity of the problem and the inevitable conflictual aspects of the process, seen from a global viewpoint.'[50] Of course, the alternative to modernization is not tradition, patriarchal relations or the old rural hierarchies, but social liberation – a modern concept that refers to the Latin American theory of dependency.

In general terms the liberation theologians and the leaders of base communities criticize the modernizing ideology of the Latin American elites (both conservative and progressive) and focus on the limits, contradictions and disasters of industrial/capitalist modernity. One of the leitmotivs of their documents is that progress in Latin America takes place at the expense of the poor. Technology as such does not take a central place in this critical discourse, which only emphasizes that in contemporary Latin American societies technological modernity and the benefits of civilization are monopolized by the State and the ruling classes. One can find, for instance, in the Brazilian CEBs – and among the pastoral agents, lay advisers, theologians and bishops who co-operate with them – a deep mistrust of the so-called 'mega-projects of development' based on modern technology: hydroelectric dams, superhighways, giant chemical or nuclear plants, huge agribusiness ventures, etc. These projects are often described as 'Pharaonic' – a biblical expression with obviously negative social and religious connotations. The projects favoured by CEBs are local co-operative ventures, with traditional or semi-modern techniques, employing little capital and much labour.

This said, however, it is true that liberationist Christianity does not have an explicit doctrine on technology. It is mainly in the social and political context that the use of modern technologies is rejected or criticized. Modern techniques are judged not by their economic results – in terms of profit, rentability, productivity, export or hard currency income – but in terms of their social consequences for the poor. If the consequences are positive – in terms of employment or life conditions – they are accepted; otherwise, they may be refused. One can find here a certain pragmatism, combined with a moral stance of religious inspiration – the preferential option for the poor is the criterion by which to evaluate technology.

Usually, rural CEBs are more sceptical than the urban ones of the benefits of modern techniques. During the last few years there have been several conflicts in Brazil around the construction of hydroelectric dams. Initially the base communities, bishops and CPT (Land Pastoral Commission) asked mainly for indemnities for the expelled peasants. For instance, a few bishops and pastoral agents from an area of conflict in the Brazilian north-east met in March 1977 and published a statement denouncing large-scale hydraulic works started by the military regime 'in the name of a progress whose result is the concentration of wealth in the hands of a privileged minority'. In their eyes, such projects were evil because, instead of helping the poor, they took away from them their last piece of land, throwing them into absolute destitution. However, at the same time the document avoided any global rejection of technical modernization: 'We do not deny the legitimacy of hydroelectric units or irrigation projects, but we condemn the manner in which these works have been implemented, without taking into consideration the dignity of human beings and the relocation of the expelled families.' In approximately the same period, in the Brazilian south, the CPT criticized the harmful consequences of the gigantic dam of Itaipu in a document significantly called *The Pharaoh's Mausoleum*, which also focused on the issues of peasant expropriation and insufficient compensation.[51]

However, during the last few years, CEBs, the CPT and their technical advisers have begun to criticize dams and other 'megaprojects' in *ecological* terms. There seems to be a certain convergence in this area between a section of the Brazilian Church – CPT, CIMI (the indigenous pastoral), and some bishops – local trade unionists, Christian and leftist intellectuals, and ecologists, around the issue of protecting the Amazonian rainforest.[52]

On the other hand, confronted with the development of modern and technologically sophisticated agribusiness (machines, pesticides, fertilizers) orientated towards export crops, CEBs and land pastorals have tried to organize rural co-operatives by making use of old traditions of collective work and communitarian mutual help.

Urban CEBs willingly mobilize for technical improvements to their life conditions: electricity, running water, sewerage, collective transportation. But they prefer solutions which come 'from the grass roots', even if their technology is primitive, to those that come from 'above' through modern technology – for instance, the construction of housing by organized mutual help. To give a typical example, the popular movement for housing in the south of Greater São Paulo imposed – against the will of the (local and regional) authorities who favoured 'highly industrialized' solutions (inevitably more expensive) – a project of building hundreds of houses through its local collectives, largely inspired by base communities, according to the method of *mutirão* ('mutual help' in Brazilian traditional language).[53]

A separate issue is the attitude of liberation theologians and the 'Church of the Poor' towards the media. There is usually a great mistrust of the institutional media (TV, radio, press), considered to be instruments of popular manipulation by the elite. The criticism of television is an important theme for liberationist Christianity, but it deals more with the content of the programmes than with the technical media themselves. However, liberation theologians –

in contrast to evangelicals and certain bishops – are reluctant to use the medium of television.

Recently, the Brazilian theologian Hugo Assmann wrote a critique of the American 'Electronic Church' and its impact in Latin America. Beyond the denunciation of what he calls the 'Christian capitalism' of the tele-evangelicals, he raises the question of the medium itself: is it not, by its own nature, a reality-fetishizing machine? His provisional conclusion is that 'religion, via TV, generates, almost inevitably, the religious legitimation of an already existent fetishism' – in so far as the reflexive participation of the TV-onlooker remains minimal. However, Assmann does not want to close himself off in an unrealistic global rejection:

> TV has come to stay: one has to learn to live with it; it is of no use to have an apocalyptic (in the sense given to this term by Umberto Eco in his book *Apocalyptic or Integrated*) and purely negative attitude towards TV – it has also an extraordinary power for the socialization of necesssary ruptures in several areas of social behaviour.[54]

One can therefore summarize the position of liberationist Christianity towards technology as follows: it is an attitude not of categorical and principled rejection, but, rather, of pragmatic, cautious and critical distance, which contrasts strongly with the technological enthusiasm of Latin American elites (managers, technocrats, the military), of the modernizing intellectuals (of both rightist and leftist tendencies) and, of course, of the evangelical Churches, as well as certain conservative Catholic sectors grouped around the project Lumen 2000.

Conclusion

Liberationist Christianity, the social movement that has its intellectual expression in liberation theology, criticizes 'really existing' modernity in Latin America (dependent capitalism) in the name of both pre-modern values and a utopian modernity (the classless society), through the socio-analytical mediation of Marxist theory, which unites the critique of the first and the promise of the second. The modern *positions* of liberation theology are inseparable from its traditional *presuppositions* – and vice versa. We have here a socio-cultural form that escapes the classic dichotomies between modernity and tradition, ethics and science, religion and the secular world. As a modern reappropriation of tradition, this cultural configuration both preserves and negates tradition and modernity, in a process of 'dialectical' synthesis. Its preferential option for the poor is the criterion by which it judges and evaluates the traditional doctrine of the Church as well as modern Western society.

This is precisely where the difference between liberation theology and the European progressive theologies lies. In a recent book, the French theologian Christian Duquoc has perceptively emphasized that the latter consider exclusion (of the poor and of Third World countries) as temporary or accidental: the future belongs to the West and to the economic, social and political progress it brings. Liberation theology, by contrast, thinks of history from the reverse viewpoint, that of the defeated and excluded, the poor (in the broad sense, including oppressed classes, races and cultures), who are the bearers of universality and redemption. Unlike the European progressive culture, it rejects the optimist view of history as progress, the evaluation of technology and of modern science as the objective conditions for this progress, and the emancipation of the individual as its main criterion. This does not mean that liberation theology rejects scientific and technical progress or the formal framework of individual liberties: it is just that it cannot accept a view of history from the standpoint of these ambivalent Western criteria.[55]

Duquoc concludes from this comparison that Rome prefers liberation theology to the progressive Western theologies emanating from the Enlightenment. Could it be that active participation by Christians in the struggle of the Latin American poor for social liberation appears in the eyes of the Vatican to be less subversive than the aspiration of Catholic European intellectuals for individual emancipation? This is far from obvious: in both cases Rome is confronted with a challenge to its authority and to the traditional power system in the Church.

In fact, liberation theology shares some basic assumptions of Western progressive culture, but it has also much in common with a different tradition – *Romanticism*. Liberationist Christianity, like other contemporary social or cultural movements (e.g. ecology), is to a large extent a Romantic movement, that is, as we saw in chapter 1, a movement that protests against key aspects of modern capitalist/industrial society in the name of pre-modern values – in this case, religion and community.

Some Brazilian authors refer to the Romantic nature of the 'Church of the Poor' and its communitarian utopia as proof of its regressive nature.[56] However, there also exists a revolutionary and/ or utopian Romanticism, whose aim is not a return to the past, an impossible restoration of pre-modern communities, but a *detour* by way of the past towards the future, the projection of past values into a new utopia. To this tradition, blending Gothic (or pre-historic) nostalgias with Enlightenment, stretching from Rousseau to William Morris, and from Ernst Bloch to José Carlos Mariátegui, liberation theology also belongs.

Liberation Theology and Marxism

For half a century, Marxism has been proscribed – under the caricatural epithet of 'atheist communism' – as the most formidable and insidious enemy of the Christian faith. The excommunication decreed by Pope Pius XII after World War II was merely the canonical sanction of the implacable and obsessive struggle that has built a wall of hostility in Latin America and throughout the world between the faithful of the Church and Marxist-orientated political movements. The breaches opened in this wall by the surprising convergence of Christianity and Marxism in Latin America during the past thirty-five years – particularly through liberation theology – have been among the most important factors of social transformation in the modern history of the hemisphere.

These developments have been a cause of concern for the Republican advisers to the President of the United States who met in Santa Fe, California, in 1980 and 1989. Faced with an unexpected phenomenon, Ronald Reagan's advisers correctly perceived the danger to capitalism, but were unable to offer any substantial explanation in their Santa Fe document produced in May 1980:

> U.S. foreign policy should begin to confront liberation theology (and not just react to it after the fact). . . . In Latin America, the role of the Church is vital to the concept of political freedom. Unfortunately, Marxist–Leninist forces have used the Church as a political weapon against private ownership and the capitalist system of production, infiltrating the religious community with ideas that are more communist than Christian.[57]

There is no need to dwell much on the gross inadequacy of such a pseudo-analysis in terms of 'infiltration': it completely fails to explain the internal dynamics of sectors of the Church, whose opposition to capitalism resulted, as we have seen, from a specific Catholic tradition, and owed very little to 'Marxist–Leninist forces' (i.e. the various sorts of communist parties and movements).

The same (or a similar) team of experts, working for President Bush, produced a second report (Santa Fe II) in 1988, with basically the same general thrust as the first, albeit in slightly more sophisticated terms. The discussion has now turned to the Gramscian tactics used by the Marxists, who have discovered that the most effective way to come to power is by 'dominating the nation's culture, which means securing a position of strong influence over religion, schools, the mass media and the universities': 'It is in this context that liberation theology should be viewed, as a political doctrine in the guise of religous belief, that is antipapal and anti-free-enterprise, aimed at weakening the independence of society in the face of state control.'[58] The complex and unique relationship between religious and political components in liberation theology is thus reduced to a mere 'disguise', a result of the Marxists' Machiavellian (or Gramscian) strategy.

A similar method can be found in the document on liberation theology presented at the Inter-American Conference of Armed Forces in December 1987 (La Plata, Argentina). Despite its significantly higher level of 'expertise' – it was probably prepared by a conservative theologian acting as adviser to the military – this text also interprets the phenomenon as part of a 'strategy of the International Communist Movement in Latin America, implemented through various modi operandi'.[59] Now, a minimum of common sense and socio-historical analysis would suffice for any serious observer to recognize that liberation theology – and the convergence of Christianity and Marxism in certain sectors of the Church – was not the result of any conspiracy, strategy, tactic, infiltration or manoeuvre by communists, Marxists, Gramscians or Leninists, but rather an internal development in the Church itself, stemming from its own tradition and culture. What needs to be explained is *why* this occurred: for what reason, at a given point in history – the early 1960s – and in a given part of the world – Latin America – a sector of the clergy and of the laity felt the need to adopt the Marxist method of interpretation and transformation of reality.

In this light, the analysis of Rome's main opponent of liberation theology, Cardinal Ratzinger, is much more interesting and insightful. According to the eminent prefect of the Holy Office for

the Doctrine of Faith, in the 1960s 'a perceptible vacuum of meaning had arisen in the Western world. In this situation, the various
forms of neo-Marxism became both a moral force and a promise
of meaning that seemed practically irresistible to students and
youth.' Moreover:

> the moral challenge of poverty and oppression presented itself in an
> ineluctable form at the very time when Europe and North America had
> attained a hitherto unknown affluence. This challenge evidently called
> for new responses that were not to be found in the existing tradition.
> The changed theological and philosophical situation was a formal
> invitation to seek the answer in a Christianity that allowed itself to be
> guided by the models of hope, scientifically grounded, put forward by
> Marxist philosophies.

The outcome was the emergence of liberation theologians 'who
fully embraced the basic Marxist approach'. If the gravity of the
danger presented by this new doctrine was underestimated, it was
'because it did not fit into any of the accepted categories of heresy;
its fundamental concern cannot be detected by the existing range
of standard questions'. There is no denying, the Cardinal concedes,
that this theology, which combines biblical exegesis with Marxist
analysis, is 'appealing' and has an 'almost flawless logic'. It seems
to respond to 'the requirements of science and the moral challenge
of our time'. This, however, does not make it any less of a threat:
'Indeed, an error is all the more dangerous, the greater the grain
of truth it contains.'⁶⁰

The question remains: why were Marxist-orientated 'models of
hope' able to seduce a small but significant sector of the Roman
Catholic Apostolic Church (as well as some Protestant groups) in
Latin America? To be able to answer, one has to investigate which
aspects or elements of the Church own's doctrine and of Marxism
might have favoured, facilitated or encouraged their convergence.

A concept that might prove enlightening in this type of analysis
is the one, already mentioned, used by Max Weber to study the
reciprocal relationship between religious forms and economic
ethos: elective affinity [*Wahlverwandtschaft*]. On the basis of
certain analogies, certain affinities, certain correspondences, two
cultural structures may – under certain historical circumstances
– enter into a relationship of attraction, of choice, of mutual
selection. This is not a unilateral process of influence but rather
a dynamic dialectic interaction which may lead in some cases to

symbiosis or even fusion. The following are some examples of possible areas of structural affinity or correspondence between Christianity and socialism:

1. As Lucien Goldmann has pointed out (see chapter 1), both reject the claim that the individual is the foundation of ethics, and criticize the individualistic world-views (liberal/rationalist, empiricist or hedonist). Religion (Pascal) and socialism (Marx) share faith in *trans-individual values*.

2. Both consider the *poor* to be victims of injustice. Obviously, there is considerable distance between the poor of Catholic doctrine and the proletariat of Marxist theory, but there is no denying a certain socio-ethical 'kinship' between them. As we saw above (p. 27), one of the first German authors to speak of the proletariat, ten years before Marx, was the Catholic and Romantic philosopher Johannes von Baader.

3. Both share *universalism* – internationalism or 'catholicism' (in its etymological sense) – that is, a doctrine and institutions that view humankind as a whole, whose substantial unity is above races, ethnic groups or nations.

4. Both assign a great value to *community*, to communal life, to the communal sharing of goods, and criticize the atomization, anonymity, impersonality, alienation and selfish competition of modern social life.

5. Both are *critical of capitalism* and of the doctrines of economic liberalism, in the name of some common good considered to be more important than the individual interests of private proprietors.

6. Both hope for a future kingdom of *justice and freedom, peace and fraternity among all humankind*.

Recognizing this affinity between the religious and the socialist utopias does not necessarily mean that one accepts the thesis presented by Nikolai Berdiaev, Karl Löwith, and many others, according to which Marxism is merely a secularized avatar of Judaeo-Christian messianism. It is obvious that these elements have entirely different meanings and functions in the two cultural systems, and that structural analogies like those above do not, in and of themselves, constitute a sufficient cause for convergence. For example, there is nothing further from the poor as construed in the Church's traditional social doctrine – as the object of charity and paternal protection – than the role of the proletariat in Marxist thinking, as the agent of revolutionary action. The correspondence outlined here did not prevent the Church from regarding socialism, communism and Marxism as 'intrinsically perverse' enemies of Christian faith – although, as we have seen, there have been individuals, groups and currents of thought within both Catholicism and the various branches of Protestantism that have been attracted to modern revolutionary theories.

What transformed these 'structural homologies' (to use Goldmann's term) into a dynamic relationship of elective affinity was a given historical conjuncture characterized by social polarization and political conflict, which began in Latin America with the triumph of the Cuban Revolution, and continued with a succession of military coups during the 1960s and 1970s: Brazil (1964), Argentina (1966), Uruguay (1971), Chile (1973), Argentina again (1976), and so on.

The combination of these events marked a new chapter in Latin American history, a period of social struggles, grass-roots movements and insurrections that have continued, in different forms, to the present day. This new stage was also marked by a renewal and an increase in influence of Marxist thought, particularly (but not exclusively) among students and intellectuals. It was in this context that a relationship of elective affinity between Christianity and Marxism developed among certain sectors of the Church and, drawing on existing analogies, led to a convergence or articulation of these two traditionally opposed cultures, resulting in some cases even in their fusion in a Marxist–Christian current of thought. In fact, the concept of elective affinity, which for Weber describes only the mutual selection and reciprocal reinforcement of distinct socio-cultural phenomena, stems from an alchemic doctrine that sought to explain the fusion of bodies in terms of the affinity of elements in their chemical composition.[61]

How does liberation theology fit into this picture? The main criticism levelled by the Roman *Instruction on Some Aspects of 'Liberation Theology'* (1984) against the new Latin American theologians was their use 'in an insufficiently critical way' of concepts 'borrowed from various currents of Marxist thought'. As a result of these concepts – particularly that of the class struggle – the 'Church of the Poor' of the Christian tradition became in liberation theology a 'class-based Church, which has become conscious of the needs of the revolutionary struggle as a stage towards liberation, and celebrates this liberation in its liturgy, which necessarily leads to calling into question the Church's sacramental and hierarchical structure'.[62]

These formulations are patently polemical; nevertheless, it is undeniable that liberation theologians have drawn analyses, concepts and viewpoints from the Marxist theoretical arsenal, and that these tools play an important role in their understanding of social reality in Latin America. By virtue of a few mere positive references to certain aspects of Marxism – independently of the content of these references – liberation theology has caused an immense upheaval in the political-cultural field; it has broken a taboo and encouraged a great number of Christians to take a fresh look not just at the theory but also at the practice of Marxists. Even when its approach was critical, it had nothing to do with the traditional anathemas against 'atheistic Marxism, the diabolical enemy of Christian civilization' – phrases common in the speeches of military dictators from Videla to Pinochet.

I mentioned earlier the historical conditions that have permitted this opening of Catholic culture to Marxist ideas. I should merely add here that Marxism, too, evolved in that period. There was the break-up of Stalinist monolithism in the wake of the Twentieth Congress of the Communist Party of the Soviet Union, and the Sino–Soviet split. In Latin America the Cuban Revolution represented, particularly during the 1960s, an indigenous and more attractive version of Marxism than the Soviet one; its widespread influence resulted in a major challenge to the Communist Parties' hegemony. Marxism ceased to be a closed and rigid system subject to the ideological authority of Moscow, and became once again a pluralist culture, a dynamic form of thought open to various viewpoints and therefore accessible to a new Christian interpretation.[63]

It is difficult to present an overall view of liberation theology's attitudes towards Marxism because, on the one hand, there is a very wide range of opinions – going from the cautious use of some elements to an attempt towards integral synthesis – and, on the other hand, a certain change has taken place between the positions expressed in the more radical period of 1968 to 1980 and today's more reserved stance – following Rome's criticisms, as well as the developments in Eastern Europe since 1989. Nevertheless, on the basis of the writings of the most representative liberation theologians (like Gutiérrez, Boff and some others) and of certain episcopal documents, one can identify certain common key reference points and debates.

Certain Latin American theologians (influenced by Althusser) refer to Marxism simply as one (or the) social science, to be used as a tool in a strictly instrumental way, in order to improve our knowledge of Latin American reality. This is at one and the same time too wide and too narrow a definition. Too wide because Marxism is not the only social science; too narrow because Marxism is not only a science but is founded on a practical choice. It aims not just at knowing the world, but at changing it.

In reality, the interest – what many authors call the 'fascination' – of many liberation theologians for Marxism is greater and more profound than the mere borrowing of a few concepts for scientific purposes would suggest.[64] It also involves Marxism's values, its ethical/political choices and its vision of a utopian future. As often happens, it is Gustavo Gutiérrez who has the most perceptive insights, emphasizing that Marxism provides not only a scientific analysis but also a utopian aspiration of social change. He criticizes the scientistic vision of Althusser, which 'prevents us from seeing the profound unity of Marx's work and consequently of easily understanding its capacity to inspire a radical and permanent revolutionary praxis'.[65]

Which sort of Marxism inspires the liberation theologians? Certainly not that of the Soviet diamat (dialectical materialism) textbooks, nor that of the Latin American Communist Parties. Rather, they are attracted to 'Western Marxism' – occasionally dubbed 'neo-Marxism' in their documents. In *Liberation Theology – Perspectives*, Gustavo Gutiérrez's great seminal work (1971), the most quoted Marxist writer is Ernst Bloch. There are also references to Althusser, Marcuse, Lukács, Gramsci, Henri Lefebvre, Lucien Goldmann and Ernest Mandel (counterposed to Althusser for his better understanding of Marx's concept of alienation).[66]

But these European references are less important than the Latin American ones: the Peruvian José Carlos Mariátegui, as the source of an original 'indo-american' Marxism, adapted to the realities of the continent; the Cuban Revolution, as a watershed in the history of Latin America, and finally dependency theory, the criticism of dependent capitalism put forward by Fernando Henrique Cardoso, André Gunder Frank, Theotonio dos Santos and Aníbal Quijano (all mentioned several times in Gutiérrez's book). It goes without saying that Gutiérrez and his co-thinkers emphasize certain Marxist themes (humanism, alienation, praxis, utopia) and reject others ('materialist ideology', atheism).[67]

This discovery of Marxism by progressive Christians and liberation theology was not a purely intellectual or academic process. The starting point for it was an unavoidable fact, a brutal mass reality in Latin America: poverty. For many socially concerned believers, Marxism was chosen because it appeared to be the most systematic, coherent and global explanation of the causes of this poverty, and the only sufficiently radical proposition for abolishing it.

Concern for the poor has been a tradition of the Church for almost two millennia, going back to the evangelical sources of Christianity. Latin American theologians place themselves in the continuity of this tradition, which provides them with both references and inspiration. But as I have already stressed several times, they break sharply with the past on a key point: for them, poor people are no longer essentially objects of charity, but agents of their own liberation. Paternalistic aid or assistance is replaced by solidarity with the poor's struggle for self-emancipation. This is where the link is made with *the* fundamental Marxist political principle: the emancipation of the workers will be the work of the workers themselves. This change is perhaps the liberation theologians' most important new political contribution. It also has the greatest consequences in the area of social praxis.

The Vatican accuses liberation theologians of having replaced the poor of Christian tradition with the Marxian proletariat. This criticism is inaccurate. For Latin American theologians, 'the poor' is a concept having moral, biblical and religious connotations. God himself is defined by them as the 'God of the Poor' and Christ is reincarnated in today's crucified poor. It is also a socially broader concept than that of the working class: it includes, according to Gutiérrez, not only the exploited classes but also the despised races and marginalized cultures – in his most recent writings he adds women, a social category that is doubly exploited.

Some Marxists will no doubt criticize this replacement of the 'materialist' concept of the proletariat by such a vague, emotional and imprecise category ('the poor'). In reality, this term corresponds to the Latin American situation, where one finds, in both the towns and the countryside, an enormous mass of poor people, including workers, but also unemployed, semi-employed, seasonal workers, street vendors, marginal people, prostitutes, and so on, who are excluded from the 'formal' productive system. The Christian/Marxist trade-union activists of El Salvador have invented a term which covers all these components of the oppressed and exploited population: the 'pooretariat' [*pobretariado*].

The preferential option for the poor, adopted by the Puebla Conference of Latin American Bishops (1979) was in practice a compromise formula, interpreted in a traditional (social assistance) sense by the Church's more moderate and conservative currents, and as a commitment to the organization and struggle of poor people for their own liberation by the liberation theologians. In other words, the Marxist class struggle, not only as 'an instrument of analysis' but as a guide for action, became an essential feature of the political/religious culture of the most radical sectors of liberationist Christianity. As Gustavo Gutiérrez stated in 1971:

> To deny the reality of the class struggle means in practice taking a position in favour of the dominant social sectors. Neutrality on this question is impossible. [What is needed is] to eliminate the appropriation by a few of the surplus value produced by the work of the great majority, and not lyrical appeals in favour of social harmony. We need to build a socialist society which is more just, more free and more humane and not a society of false conciliation and apparent equality.

This led him to the following practical conclusion: 'Building a just society today necessarily means being consciously and actively involved in the class struggle taking place in front of us.'[68]

How can this be squared with the Christian obligation of universal love? Gutiérrez's answer is distinguished by its great political rigour and moral generosity: we do not hate our oppressors, we want to liberate them, too, by freeing them from their own alienation, their ambition, their egoism – in a word, from their inhumanity. But to do that, we must resolutely choose the side of the oppressed and concretely and effectively fight the oppressor class.

To fight effectively against poverty one must understand its causes. This is where liberation theology converges again with Marxism. As the well-known Brazilian cardinal Dom Helder Câmara once said: 'As long as I asked people to help the poor, I was called a saint. But when I asked the question: why is there so much poverty? I was called a communist.' The poverty of the great majority and the incredible wealth of the privileged few are underpinned by the same economic foundation – *dependent capitalism*, the domination of the economy by the multinational corporations.

In the 1960s the anti-capitalist ethical tradition of the Church started to be articulated within the Marxist analysis of capitalism – which also includes a moral condemnation of injustice – specifically in the form of dependency theory. The great merit of dependency theorists, notably André Gunder Frank and Aníbal Quijano, was to break with the 'developmentist' illusions that prevailed among Latin American Marxists in the 1950s, by showing that the cause of misery, underdevelopment, growing inequality and military dictatorships was not 'feudalism' or insufficient modernization, but the very structure of dependent capitalism. Consequently, they argued that only some form of socialist transformation could wrest Latin American nations from dependency and poverty. Certain aspects of this analysis were to be integrated not only by the liberation theologians but also by some bishops and episcopal conferences, particularly in Brazil.[69]

Does this mean that the Church has been infiltrated by communist ideas, as the US Republican experts wrote in 1980? If by 'communist ideas' one means those of the Communist Parties, then this statement completely misses the point. Liberationist Christianity, inspired in the first place by religious and ethical considerations, displays a much more radical, intransigent and categorical anti-capitalism – since it includes the dimension of moral revulsion – than the Latin American Communist Parties, who still believe in the progressive virtues of the industrial bourgeoisie and the historical 'anti-feudal' role of industrial (capitalist) development. One example will suffice to illustrate this paradox. The Brazilian Communist Party explained in its Sixth Congress resolutions (1967): 'The socialization of the means of production does not correspond to the present level of the contradiction between the productive forces and the relations of production.'[70] In other words, industrial capitalism must first develop the economy and modernize the country, before one can start talking about socialism. However, in 1973, the bishops and superiors of religious orders of the Centre-West region of Brazil published a document entitled *The Cry of the Churches*, with the following conclusion:

> We must overcome capitalism: it is the greatest evil, an accumulated sin, the rotten roots, the tree which produces all the fruit we know so well: poverty, hunger, illness and death. . . . In order to do this it is necessary to go beyond private ownership of the means of production (factories, land, commerce and banks).[71]

Another episcopal document is even more explicit. *The Declaration of the Bishops of the North-East of Brazil* (1973) states:

> The injustice produced by this society is the fruit of capitalist relations of production which necessarily create a class society characterized by discrimination and injustice. . . . The oppressed class has no other option for its liberation than to follow the long and difficult road (the journey has already begun) leading to the social ownership of the means of production. This is the principal foundation of the gigantic historical project of the global transformation of present society into a new society in which it becomes possible to create the objective conditions allowing the oppressed to recover the humanity they have been stripped of. . . . The Gospel calls all Christians and all men of good will to join this prophetic current.[72]

The document was signed by thirteen bishops (including Dom Helder Câmara), by the provincial superiors of the Franciscans, Jesuits and Redemptionists, and by the abbot of the Benedictine monastery in Bahía.

As one can see from these episcopal documents – and many similar ones that have come out of the liberationist Christian current – solidarity with the poor leads to a condemnation of capitalism and sometimes even to an aspiration towards socialism. What sort of socialism? This is not a topic much discussed by liberation theologians, who prefer to deal with general ethics and social values rather than with strategical and tactical issues, which are left to the political movements to take care of. There was, however, a more or less explicit criticism of the so-called 'really existing' models of socialism – well before 1989 – among liberationist Christians. For instance, Gutiérrez insisted that the oppressed people of Latin America must leave the previously adopted paths and creatively seek their own road to socialism. His approach is inspired by José Carlos Mariátegui, for whom (writing in the 1920s) socialism in Latin America cannot be a 'pure imitation' or 'copy' of other experiences, but must be a 'heroic creation': 'We must give birth, through our own reality, our own language, to an Indo-American socialism.'[73] It goes without saying that, for liberation theologians, socialism, or any form of human emancipation, is only a preparation for or anticipation of total salvation, of the coming of the Kingdom of God on earth.

We should not deduce from all this that liberation theologians 'adhere' to Marxism. As Leonardo and Clodovis Boff emphasize in their answer to Cardinal Ratzinger, Marxism is used as a mediation for the renewal of theology:

> It has helped clarify and enrich certain major theological notions: the people, the poor, history and even praxis and politics. That does not mean to say that we have reduced the theological content of these notions to the limits of the Marxist form. On the contrary, we have used the valid theoretical content (which conforms to the truth) of Marxist notions within the theological horizon.[74]

Among those aspects of Marxism they reject are, as one might expect, materialist philosophy and atheist ideology; but that does not seem to be a matter of great concern to them, since they consider not atheism but idolatry to be the main adversary of Christianity in Latin America. More important is their rejection of the economistic tendency in Marxism, particularly of the 'developmentist' brand, with its blinkered culture of 'economic progress', 'modernization', and the 'development of productive forces' at any cost.

Marxist partisans of modernization often brand liberationist Christians as 'populists' because of their sympathy for certain pre-capitalist traditions of communitarian life and mutual help, kept alive in popular culture (particularly among peasants), and because of their tendency to replace the proletariat as the unique subject of emancipation by broader concepts: 'the poor', 'the people', including the peasantry and the indigenous communities. For instance, the well-known Brazilian Marxist anthropologist Otavio Guilherme Velho criticized the Brazilian Church for 'considering the process of capitalist development as an absolute evil', and for insisting on 'a total opposition between its conception of land and the "capitalist" one'. By reproducing a spontaneous peasant ideology based on the pre-capitalist past, the Church is unable to confront such basic issues as the need for a bourgeois revolution. The Church's stance on the agrarian question has much in common with the Russian populist tradition, in opposition to orthodox Marxism for which 'capitalist development is seen not as an absolute evil, but as a precondition for future transformations'. Of course, not all Latin American Marxists share this very 'classical' standpoint, but this essay is representative of a significant current among leftist modernizers. It is an old debate in Latin American Marxism: because of his call for an 'Indo-American socialism' based on the indigenous communitarian tradition (what he called 'Inca communism'), José Carlos Mariátegui had already been denounced by Soviet Marxists and their Latin American followers as a 'romanticist' and a 'populist'.[75]

Of course, liberation theologians cannot accept the Marxian characterization of religion as the 'opium of the people'. However, they do not entirely reject Marxist criticism of the Church and of 'really existing' religious practices. For instance, Gustavo Gutiérrez acknowledged that the Latin American Church has contributed to giving a sacred character to the established order: 'The protection it receives from the social class that benefits from and defends the capitalist society that prevails in Latin America, has made the institutionalized Church a part of the system, and the Christian message a component of ruling ideology.'[76] This severe judgement is shared by a sector of the Latin American bishops. For example, the Peruvian bishops, in a declaration adopted by their Thirty-sixth Episcopal Assembly (1969) stated: 'Above all, we Christians should recognize that through lack of faith we have contributed in our words and actions, by our silence and omissions, to the present situation of injustice.'

One of the most interesting documents on this question is a resolution adopted by the CELAM Department of Education towards the end of the 1960s (before the institution came under conservative hegemony):

> The Christian religion has been used and is still used as an ideology justifying the rule of the powerful. Christianity in Latin America has been a functional religion for the system. Its rites, its churches and its work have contributed to channelling the people's dissatisfaction towards the beyond, totally disconnected from the present world. Thus Christianity has held back the people's protest against an unjust and oppressive system.[77]

Of course, this criticism is made in the name of an authentic Christianity, in solidarity with the poor and oppressed, and has nothing in common with a materialist questioning of religion as such.

As these extracts from the theologians' writings and bishops' pronouncements show, a significant but minority sector of the Latin American Church has tacitly integrated certain basic Marxist tenets into its new understanding of Christianity. Some Christian trade unionists or members of left-wing organizations, as well as some radical movements like Christians for Socialism, have taken a further step by attempting a synthesis or fusion between Christianity and Marxism. Here we are talking about a Christian current inside the revolutionary movement. Indeed, as we shall see in the next chapters, in many places (for example, in Brazil, Central America) it is one of the main components of the revolutionary movement.

The problem of a tactical alliance with the so-called Left Christian forces has been part of the concerns of the labour movement and Marxists in Latin America (and elsewhere) for a long time. During his trip to Chile in 1971, Fidel Castro mentioned the possibility of passing from a tactical to a strategic alliance between Marxists and Christians. But today, after the experiences of Brazil, Nicaragua and El Salvador, one should no longer be speaking in terms of an alliance but rather of organic unity. For the Christians are already one of the essential components of the labour and revolutionary movement in many countries of Latin America.

Marxists reacted in different ways to this new and unexpected development. While some tended to assess it as a clerical trick or as a new form of the 'opium for the people', others were willing to adopt a more open-minded attitude, and accept revolutionary Christians as legitimate members of the movement. A good example is Comandante Luis Carrión, a member of the national leadership of the FSLN, who perceptively summarized the issue in an interview given in August 1985:

> I see no obstacle which should prevent Christians, without renouncing their faith, from making their own all the Marxist conceptual tools which are required for a scientific understanding of the social processes and a revolutionary orientation in political practice. In other words, a Christian can be at once a Christian and a perfectly consistent Marxist. . . . In this sense, our experience can teach many lessons. Many Christians have been and are active in the Sandinista Front and some of them are even priests. And I am not speaking here only of rank-and-file militants: some of them are members of the Sandinista Assembly and hold high political responsibilities. . . . I think that certain Marxist vanguards have had a tendency to perceive progressive and revolutionary Christian sectors as an opponent force competing for a fraction of the political following of these parties. I think this is a mistake. Avoiding that mistake is one of the great achievements of the FSLN. We have linked up with the grass-roots structures of the Church, not to pull people out of them, but to integrate them into the Sandinista Front as a stage in its political development, without this meaning in any way that we oppose their participation in Christian institutions. On the

contrary, we leave people in these structures so that their higher commitment will be transformed into political action in this environment. We never told them that in joining the FSLN they had to face the dilemma of the Christian faith or their activity in the Front. If we had posed things in that way, we would have remained a tiny group of activists.[78]

It should be stressed, however, that outside Brazil and Central America most members of the 'Church of the Poor' are reluctant to engage in a significant relation with Marxism; this is not only because of the Vatican's campaign, but also because of a more general mistrust of theory and overtly political commitment. Moreover, some of the theologians who once often used Marxist categories are now much more cautious, particularly since the European events of 1989 (the inglorious end of the Soviet bloc). One can say that today there exists a general tendency to de-emphasize the relationship of liberationist Christianity to Marxism.

3

Politics and Religion in Latin America: Three Examples

The Brazilian Church and Politics

The Brazilian Church is a unique case in Latin America, in so far as it is the only Church on the continent where liberation theology and its pastoral followers have won a decisive influence. The importance of this fact is obvious, considering that this is the largest Catholic Church in the world. Moreover, the new Brazilian popular movements – the radical trade-union confederation (CUT), the landless peasant movements (MST), the poor neighbourhood associations – and their political expression, the new Workers' Party (Partido dos Trabalhadores – PT), are to a significant extent the product of the grass-roots activity of committed Christians, lay pastoral agents and Christian base communities.

Two examples illustrate how radical was the historical change in the Church's social and political position.

Gregorio Bezerra, a well-known Brazilian communist leader, tells in his memoirs how, during a meeting in a small town in the north-east around 1946 (when the Communist Party was legalized), he was threatened by a fanatical mob, led by the local priest, shouting, 'Death to communism! Long live Christ the King!' The communist leader was forced to run for his life and finally took refuge at the local police headquarters, in order to escape from this obscurantist horde. Thirty-five years later, we had exactly the reverse scenario: during a metalworkers' strike in 1980, a demonstration by trade unionists of São Bernardo (an industrial suburb of São Paulo) was attacked by the police, and the demonstrators were forced to take refuge at the church, which was opened by the bishop in order to receive them.

How did this change take place? By the late 1950s one could already perceive the emergence of different currents among the bishops and the clergy. The three most influential were the traditionalists, the conservative modernizers and the reformists: all shared a common repulsion for 'atheistic communism'. The most progressive figure was Dom Helder Câmara, Archbishop of Olinda, who represented the 'theology of development' at its best, and raised the issue of the dramatic poverty among the people of the north-east.

In the early 1960s, however, there appeared an entirely new tendency, soon to be known as the 'Catholic Left'. Under the influence of recent French theology, of Father Lebret's humanist economics and Emmanuel Mounier's personalist socialism – as well as the Cuban Revolution – the Catholic student movement, the JUC, became radicalized and moved very quickly towards leftist and socialist ideas. In a pioneering document presented in 1960, *Some Guidelines for a Historical Ideal for the Brazilian People*, several leaders of the JUC denounced the evils of capitalism:

> We have to say, without ambiguity or hesitation, that capitalism, historically realized, deserves only the calm condemnation of Christian consciousness. Is it necessary to justify this? It will be enough to recall here some of the alienations of human nature characteristic of the concrete capitalist situation: reduction of human labour to the condition of a commodity; dictatorship of private property, not subordinated to the demands of the common good; abuses of economic power; unbridled competition on one side, and monopolistic practices of all kinds on the other; central motivation as the pursuit of profit. The humanity of the worker cannot remain, in Brazilian society, submissive to the tyranny of money and of cruel competition, in short to the mechanisms of capitalism.

The Catholic students called for the 'replacement of the anarchic economy, based on profit, by an economy organized according to humane principles' – an aim which in practice requires the 'nationalization of the basic productive sectors'. The document contains quotes from Thomas Aquinas, Pope Leo XIII and Emmanuel Mounier, as well as references to traditional Catholic doctrines (the common good, natural law), but it also uses Marxist concepts and points towards the need for a socialist transformation of Brazilian society. Trying to formulate 'an essentially anti-capitalist and anti-imperialist ideology' and searching for a 'more just and humane social structure', it calls for an 'effective commitment to the exploited class, in an effective negation of the capitalist structure'.[1]

One can define the spirit of this seminal and pioneering document – perhaps the first example of liberationist Christian thinking in Latin America – as a *sui generis* combination of the traditional Catholic, the personalist (Mounier) and the Marxist critique of capitalism, in the context of an 'underdeveloped' country. The antipathy – or negative affinity – to capitalism, considered to be 'a monstruous structure, based on all kinds of abuses, exploitations and crimes against the dignity of humans', has a strong ethical/religious flavour, which sharply distinguishes this Christian Left from the hegemonic tendencies in the secular Brazilian Left at the time.

Using several components of French progressive Catholic culture, the Brazilian Christian Left – i.e. the various youthful branches of Catholic Action (JEC, JUC, JOC), the Dominicans, some Jesuits and some Catholic intellectuals – from the early 1960s began to create a radically new form of religious thought and practice. In his interesting book on the Catholic Church and politics in Brazil, Scott Mainwaring writes on this issue:

> Progressive European theologians (like Maritain, Lebret, Congar, Mounier) had an influence at the beginning of this process, but the Catholic Left did much more than introduce European social thought into the Brazilian Church. They applied the European ideas to the Brazilian conditions and developed a new conception of the Church's mission.

This analysis seems to me to be insufficient: what the Brazilians did was not to 'apply' to Brazil a body of French ideas, but to use them as a starting point to create new ideas, to invent a political-religious culture – one cannot yet speak of a 'theology' in the strict meaning of the word – of specifically Brazilian inspiration. These ideas and practices of the years 1960–62 may be considered as the birth of an authentically *Latin American* Christian thought/action ('see, judge, act', according to the well-known formula of Catholic Action).[2]

The internal logic of this reinterpretation and change in relation to the French reference can be summarized in one word: *radicalization*. It consisted in a selection of the most advanced positions in French writings (often taken out of their original context), a growing incorporation of Marxist elements, and a radical change of perspective, replacing the European angle with the viewpoint of the oppressed periphery of the world capitalist system. This radicalization was intimately linked to new social, cultural and political practices of the Catholic activists: participation in the student movement, often in alliance with the secular Left, support for social struggles; and commitment to popular education.

This last aspect was surely one of the most important: during the early 1960s, Catholic activists, with the support of the Church, formed the Movement for Base Education (MEB) which was the first Catholic attempt at a radical pastoral practice among the popular classes. Under the guidance of Paulo Freire's pedagogy, MEB aimed not only to bring literacy to the poor, but to raise their consciousness and to help them become the agents of their own history. In 1962 JUC and MEB activists created Popular Action (Ação Popular – AP), a non-confessional political movement committed to the struggle for socialism and to using the Marxist method.

The Brazilian Catholic Left of the 1960s was a true forerunner of liberationist Christianity. However, unlike the Church of the Poor in the 1970s, it had a limited mass following and soon it was attacked and de-legitimated by the hierarchy, who denounced JUC leftist leanings as opposed to the sane social doctrine of the Church. After 1964 AP moved away not only from the Church but also from Christianity (although it still enjoyed the support of many Christians, both lay and clerical), and the majority of its members joined the Maoist Partido Comunista do Brasil (PCdoB).

In April 1964, the military took power, in order to save 'Western Christian civilization' from 'atheistic communism', that is, to defend the ruling oligarchy threatened by the rise of social movements under the elected president, João Goulart. In June 1964, after two months of reflection, the Bishops' Conference (Conferencia Nacional dos Bispos Brasileiros – CNBB) issued a statement supporting the coup:

> In answer to the anxious and general expectations of the Brazilian people, who saw the accelerated march of communism towards the conquest of power, the armed forces intervened in time, and prevented the establishment of a Bolshevik regime in our country. . . . While giving thanks to God, who answered the prayers of millions of Brazilians and freed us from the communist danger, we are grateful to the military, who, at serious risk to their lives, rose up in the name of the supreme interests of the nation.

By this argument – ecclesiastical legitimation of military coups in Latin America – the Church gave its blessing to the establishment of a military regime that would suppress democratic freedoms in Brazil for the next twenty years.[3]

In spite of the new openings advocated by John XXIII and by the first debates of the Vatican II Council, as well as the support of many Brazilian bishops for social reforms, in a critical conjuncture the Church chose the camp of the anti-democratic, authoritarian and conservative forces, in the name of outworn Cold War arguments: a purely imaginary 'Bolshevik danger' in Brazil.

If this stance seemed to enjoy the support of the whole episcopal body – including its most progressive component, represented by Dom Helder Câmara – it was far from being accepted by the Christian activists of JEC, JUC, JOC and of Catholic Action in general (as well as the priests and religious working with them), many of whom were among the first victims of the witch-hunt launched by the new authorities.

Intially, the Christian Left was broken down by repression and marginalized. However, during the next few years, with the rise of opposition to the dictatorship in civil society, a growing number of Catholics (as well as Protestants, of course), including priests, religious, nuns and even a few bishops, began to side with the opposition. Some of them became radicalized and, during 1967–68, a large group of Dominicans decided to support armed resistance and to help clandestine movements such as the ALN (Action for National Liberation) – a guerrilla group founded by a former leader of the Communist Party, Carlos Marighella – by hiding its members or helping some of them to escape the country. Soon several of them would be imprisoned and tortured by the military, and the guerrilla movement destroyed.

As in a upward-moving spiral, the participation of Christian activists in actions considered to be subversive was followed by a repression that became increasingly brutal – imprisonments, rapes, tortures, murders – against Church people, and even members of the clergy (particularly of the religious orders), especially after the Institutional Act no. 5, of December 1968, which abolished the remaining civil liberties and juridical guarantees.

The Church's hierarchy was at first rather cautious, at the same time disposed to co-operate with the military government but favourable to a gradual return to a constitutional order. Even after the murder of a priest, Henrique Pereira Neto, adviser to the

Catholic students in Recife, in May 1969, and the terrifying information about tortures inflicted upon the imprisoned religious (mainly Dominicans) and nuns, the bishops hesitated to take a stand against the regime. Dom Agnelo Rossi, the Archbishop of São Paulo – the greatest diocese in Brazil – visited the military president, General Garrastazú Médici, in November 1969, to express 'his sincere wishes for the success of his governement' and the desire of the Church to 'keep cordial relations with the government, in order to join forces for the benefit of the country'.[4] According to Scott Mainwaring:

> his entire tenure as archbishop of São Paulo (1964–70) was marked by a reluctance to criticize the regime, by efforts to deny the existence of Church–state conflict, and by continual attempts to negotiate with the regime. He was among the few prominent archbishops who continued to say mass to commemorate the coup, and on several trips abroad he argued that reports of torture were exaggerated.[5]

Others, like the auxiliary Bishop of São Paulo, Lucas Moreira Neves, asked by the Provincial of the Dominican Order to give testimony on the torture suffered by the religious Frei Tito de Alencar, refused to speak because this would 'harm his pastoral activities'.[6]

Meanwhile, the scandal of torture in Brazilian prisons, and the fact that numerous Catholics (lay activists or clergy) were among the victims, began to touch international Catholic opinion, and even the Roman Curia: statements were made by the Vatican's Peace and Justice Commission and even, more discreetly, by Pope Paul VI himself (without explicitly mentioning Brazil). In May 1970, while visiting Paris, Dom Helder Câmara openly denounced the use of torture in Brazil for the first time, and immediately became the object of a vicious campaign by the Brazilian authorities and the conformist press, accusing him of 'slandering our fatherland among foreigners'. São Paulo's governor, Abreu Sodré, went so far as to call him 'a Fidel Castro in a cassock' who 'belongs to the propaganda machine of the Communist Party'.

At the end of May 1970, a meeting of the CNBB took place in Brasilia and a pastoral document was issued that took up a position, in a most cautious way, in the debate: while condemning, in principle, any use of torture, it declared that the juridical verification of the denunciations in this respect was 'beyond our competence'. It even proclaimed its conviction that 'if such facts were proved, they would hardly correspond to an official policy of the government'. The pro-military press did not fail to celebrate this document as a victory for the regime.[7]

However, as the outrage of international and Brazilian Catholic opinion increased, such a position became untenable. Everything began to change a few months later: in October 1970 (soon after Paul VI's speech against torture), Dom Agnelo Rossi was 'promoted' to a high position in Rome and replaced by a new bishop, Dom Paulo Evaristo Arns, well known for his commitment to the defence of human rights and his solidarity with the imprisoned religious. Soon afterwards the CNBB elected a new president, Dom Aloisio Lorscheider, who moved the Church into an increasingly open opposition to the military dictatorship.

The change was so profound that during the 1970s, after the wiping out of the underground Left, the Church appeared, in the eyes of civil society and of the military themselves, as the main adversary of the authoritarian state – a much more powerful (and radical) enemy than the tolerated (and tame) parliamentarian opposition, the MDB, Brazilian Democratic Movement. Various social movements, in defence of human rights or of workers' and peasants' unions, found refuge under the Church's protective umbrella. Through the voice of its bishops, the Church criticized, in an increasingly direct and explicit way the violations of human rights and the absence of democracy. But that was not all: it also denounced the mode of development imposed by the military, its whole programme of 'modernization', as inhuman, unjust, and based on the social and economic oppression of the poor.

For instance, in 1973, the bishops and provincial leaders of the various religious orders in the North-East and Centre-West areas of Brazil issued two statements which denounced not only the dictatorship but also what they called 'the root of evil': capitalism. These documents were, as a matter of fact, the most radical statements ever issued by a group of bishops anywhere in the world (we have seen some passages from them at pp. 75–6). The pattern of economic development imposed by the regime and the ruling classes – and in particular the savage capitalism expanding in the rural areas and expelling the peasants from their land – came under growing critical fire from the CNBB. The Church was denounced by the top brass of the Army as subversive and Marxist-inspired – as well as utopian, feudal and backward, because of its opposition to 'modernization' and (capitalist) 'progress'.

Also during this period, the ecclesiastical base communities (CEBs) began to grow, under the impetus of a large number of priests and religious, and with the support of the radical bishops. The female religious orders were not only the most numerous – there are thirty-seven thousand nuns in Brazil – but also the single most effective factor in the promotion of communities in the poor urban neighbourhoods. As a result, at the end of the decade there existed tens of thousands of such base communities, with hundreds of thousands (perhaps a few million) participants.[8]

Common suffering (poverty) and hopes of redemption were the key components of the political/religious culture of the Brazilian base communities, very much as described by Max Weber when formulating the ideal-type of the *Gemeindereligiosität*:

> The principle that constituted communal relations among the salvation prophecies was the suffering common to all believers. . . . The more imperatives that issued from the ethic of reciprocity among neighbours were raised, the more rational the conception of salvation became, and the more it was sublimated into an ethic of absolute ends. Externally, such commands rose to a communism of loving brethren [*brüderlichen Liebeskommunismus*]; internally they rose to the attitude of *caritas*, love for the sufferer *per se*, for one's neighbour, for man, and finally for the enemy.[9]

During these years, one can also see the emergence of a new cultural and religious force: Brazilian liberation theology. Its first representative was, as mentioned above, Hugo Assmann, who began to link Christian motives with the Marxist philosophy of praxis. Inspired by his experience of work among the urban poor, and by his profound knowledge of Marxism – both European (Frankfurt!) and Latin American (dependency theory) – Assmann's writings of 1970–71 are among the most radical and coherent documents produced about liberation theology. Assmann was forced into exile, but soon other theologians emerged: the best-known are the two brothers Leonardo and Clodovis Boff, who belonged to the Franciscan and the Redemptorist Orders respectively. Through their writings and through the progressive Catholic publishing house Vozes, in Petropolis, they provided spiritual and political guidance to the Church people, and educated a whole generation of pastoral agents, base community leaders, seminar students and Catholic intellectuals. Highly creative and original minds, out-spoken in their use of Marxist categories, Leonardo and Clodovis were supported by several Brazilian bishops who were sympathetic to their ideas. In 1992, confronted with growing restrictions and censorship from Rome, Leonardo Boff decided to leave the Franciscan Order and become a lay theologian.

The CEBs and the pastoral activists of the Church – belonging to the workers' pastoral, the land pastoral, the *favela* (shantytown) pastoral, the youth pastoral – provided a significant part of the grass-roots constituency for the new social and political movements that arose during the gradual re-democratization of the country in the 1980s: (a) the new Workers' Party, founded in 1980, whose candidate, the metalworkers' union leader Luis Inacio da Silva ('Lula'), almost won the presidential elections in 1989 (he got 47 per cent of the vote); (b) the United Workers' Congress (CUT), the new class-struggle trade-union federation, founded in 1983, which quickly became hegemonic in the labour movement, organizing around ten million urban and rural workers; (c) the Landless Peasants' Movement (MST), which has promoted massive land occupations in various areas of the country; (d) the National Co-ordination of Popular Movements (recently created), a loose federation of neighbourhood and other local movements.

It is true, as I have already mentioned, that among many CEBs people and pastoral agents there is often a very strong *basista* tendency, leading to localism, a slow pace of organization, mistrust of 'outsiders' and intellectuals, and a low level of politicization. This has been criticized by liberation theologians (like Clodovis Boff and Frei Betto) and Marxist activists. But it should also be stressed that the base communities helped to create a new political culture in Brazil, the 'grass-roots democracy', in opposition not only to military authoritarianism, but also to the three main political traditions of the country: clientelism – traditionally practised in the rural areas by the landowners and in the urban centers by professional politicians who distribute favours (jobs, money); populism, which under Vargas and his followers permitted them to organize 'from above' the trade-union and popular movement; and verticalism, often used by the main forces of the 'old' Left, following the Soviet or Chinese example. Thanks to this new culture, CEB activists, with the support of radical theologians and bishops, contributed to the building of the largest and most radical mass (urban and rural) labour movement in the history of Brazil.

Why is it that the Brazilian Church became, from 1970 until 1995, the most advanced in the continent, the first in which leftist ideas emerged (since 1960), and the only one in which liberation theology enjoyed such a wide influence?

It is difficult to give a clear-cut answer to this question. There are several factors which have to be taken into consideration, and whose combination produced the unique characteristics of Brazilian Catholicism:

1. The growing insufficiency of the clergy, too small to control the vast and quickly expanding population of the country. This resulted in the growing influence and importance of the lay members, and in particular of Catholic Action – which was precisely the dynamic factor in the radicalization of the 1960s.

2. The strong influence of the French Catholic Church and culture on Brazil – in contrast to the rest of the continent, where the Spanish (and Italian) tradition was predominant. As we saw above, it is in France that one finds the most progressive, critical and advanced Catholic culture (including a significant leftist current). Given the direct links between French and Brazilian religious orders (particularly the Dominicans), the great number of French missionaries in Brazil and the traditional influence of French Catholic intellectuals on their Brazilian counterparts, there existed in the Brazilian Church a cultural environment much more receptive to new radical ideas than in the other Latin American countries.

3. The military dictatorship established in 1964. By progressively closing all institutional channels for the expression of popular protest (particularly after 1968), the military regime ended up transforming the Church into the last refuge of opposition. The popular movements went in vast numbers to the Church and helped to 'convert' it to the cause of the poor's liberation. At the same time, the brutal repression by the military of the radical sectors of the Church forced the institution as a whole to react and created a dynamic of permanent conflict between the State and the Church.

It should, however, be stressed that the military regime is not in itself a sufficient explanation, since in other countries (Argentina!) the dictatorship enjoyed the whole-hearted support of the Church. Although the Brazilian bishops supported the military coup of 1964, the presence of a significant radical current created the conditions for the change in 1970.

4. The speed and depth of capitalist development since the

1950s have been much greater in Brazil than in the other Latin American countries. The dizzying intensity of urbanization and industrialization, and the swiftness and brutality of capitalist expansion in the rural areas, created such an aggravation of social contradictions – such as growing social inequality, the expulsion of the rural population from the land, the massive concentration of poor dwellers on the urban periphery – that they certainly contributed to the upsurge of liberationist Christianity as a radical answer to this disastrous model of capitalist 'modernization'.

5. The radical priests and theologians of the 1970s and the 1980s, learning the lessons from the the 1960s – and from what happened in some Latin-American countries – opted for patient work inside the institution, trying not to cut themselves off from the bishops – therefore being able to win some of them over to liberation theology – and avoiding initiatives which could have led to their isolation and marginalization. Without concessions on their basic options, they refused a dynamic of internal confrontation with the hierarchy, and concentrated their efforts on developing grass-roots organization, base communities and popular pastorals.

The best way to describe the history of the radical current of the Brazilian Church is, perhaps, to tell the story of a figure who played a key role in developing the political awareness of the base communities: Frei Betto, a Dominican religious known worldwide since he published a series of talks with Fidel Castro on religion, which have been translated into fourteen languages and have gone through multiple editions in Latin America.

Born in 1944 in the city of Belo Horizonte (State of Minas Gerais), Betto, whose real name is Carlos Alberto Libânio Christo, became a leader of the Catholic Student Youth (JEC) in the early 1960s. He then entered the Dominican Order as a novice; at the time, the Order was one of the main places where a liberationist interpretation of Christianity was being elaborated. Shocked by the poverty of the people and the military dictatorship established by the coup of 1964, he linked up with a network of Dominicans who actively sympathized with the guerrilla movement. When repression intensified in 1969, Betto helped many revolutionary activists to hide or quietly cross the border into Uruguay and Argentina. This activity earned him a prison sentence from the military regime, which he served from 1969 to 1973.

In a fascinating book published recently in Brazil – *Blood Baptism. The Dominicans and the Death of Carlos Marighella* – of which more than ten editions have been printed already, he reviews this period at length, sketching the portrait of the ALN leader assassinated by the police in 1969, and that of his Dominican friends caught in the claws of the repressive machine, imprisoned and subjected to torture.[10]

The last chapter is dedicated to the tragic figure of Frei Tito de Alencar, so atrociously tortured by the Brazilian police that, even after his release from jail, he could not recover his psychic balance. In exile in France, he still believed himself persecuted by his tormentors and eventually committed suicide in August 1974.

As soon as he was released from prison in 1973, Frei Betto devoted himself to organizing base communities; in the next few years, he published several pamphlets that explained in simple and accessible language the meaning of liberation theology and the role of the CEBs. He soon became one of the main leaders of the national inter-Church gatherings at which base communities from all over Brazil exchanged their social, political and religious experiences. In 1980 he organized the Fourth International Congress of Third World Theologians.

Since 1979 Frei Betto has been in charge of the workers' pastoral at São Bernardo do Campo, an industrial suburb of São Paulo, the birthplace of the new Brazilian trade unionism. Although he has not officially joined any political organization, he does not hide his sympathies for the Workers' Party and his friendship for its president, Luis Inacio da Silva ('Lula'), the former leader of the São Bernardo metalworkers' union. During the last election (1994) he helped to create an ecumenic committee of religious personalities of various confessions to support Lula's presidential candidature.

Although the Pope seemed to support the Brazilian Church in his 1986 letter to the bishops, the Vatican's policy during the last ten years has been a systematic attempt to 'normalize' it (in the sense of the word as it was used to describe relations between the Soviet Union and Czechoslovakia after 1969). As the French Jesuit Charles Antoine wrote in a recent article, the aim of this policy is to 'dismantle' the Brazilian Church by nominating conservative bishops who often destroy or weaken the pastoral structures established by their predecessors. The best-known example is the nomination of

Monsignor José Cardoso, a conservative who specializes in canonic law and who lived in Rome from 1957 to 1979, to the place left vacant by Dom Helder Câmara. Once nominated, Monsignor Cardoso dismissed most of the leaders of the rural and popular pastorals of his diocese.[11]

Rome's aim was to change the majority in the Brazilian Conference of Bishops, which had been, since 1971, in the hands of the progressive wing of the Church. This objective was finally achieved in May 1995, with the election, to the head of the CNBB, of a conservative figure enjoying the Pope's support: Lucas Moreira Neves, Archbishop of Salvador – the one who refused to raise his voice against torture in 1969. Strongly opposed to liberation theology, Dom Lucas worked for thirteen years at the Roman Curia, and his main priorities are not poverty and social exclusion, but sexual morals: the struggle against contraception, abortion and divorce.[12]

This election is certainly a watershed and a turning point in the history of the Brazilian Church. For the moment the CEBs and the popular pastorals – particularly the land pastoral, CPT, and the Indian pastoral, CIMI – still enjoy the support of many bishops, and continue to have a large following. Moreover, even where the bishops are hostile, as in Recife, the progressive militants have been able to establish relatively autonomous organizations, such as the Centre Dom Helder Câmara (CENDHEC). However, there is no doubt that the Church will no longer play the same social and political role as during the last twenty-five years, and that liberationist Christianity will meet with growing hostility from the hierarchy. The two generations that have become radicalized during the last thirty-five years are not going to give up easily their social commitment, and many are probably going to leave the Church for lay social movements and parties – a tendency that had already begun some years ago.

Christianity and the Origins of Insurgency in Central America

Liberation Christianity arrived much later in Central America than in Brazil. However, owing to the explosive social and political situation in various countries in the region, it contributed – to some extent involuntarily – to the rise of popular insurgency, in different forms, in Nicaragua and El Salvador (as well as, to a lesser extent, in Guatemala). In both cases the political conflict induced an internal conflict in the Church, between the hierarchy and the base communities (Nicaragua) or among the bishops themselves (El Salvador). In both countries the religious orders – particularly the Jesuits and the Maryknolls – were leading forces in the process of popular 'conscientization' that prepared the ground for rebellion.

Christianity and Sandinismo in Nicaragua (1968–79)

The Nicaraguan Revolution is the first in modern times (since 1789) in which Christians – lay people and clergy – played an essential role, both at the grass-roots and at leadership levels of the movement. This cannot be explained without taking into account the previous rise of liberationist Christianity, which substantially changed the religious culture of significant sections of the Church. The Nicaraguan experience is an interesting example – although an extreme one – of interaction between politics and religion, leading to a strong cultural symbiosis, mutual influence and practical convergence in the religious culture of many believers, between Christian ethics and revolutionary hopes. For the reasons mentioned above (chapter 2), religious orders and foreign priests were pioneering elements in this historical development.

Before the Medellín Conference (1968), the Nicaraguan Church was a rather traditionalist and socially conservative institution, which openly supported the Somoza dynasty. In 1950 its bishops issued a statement proclaiming that all authority derives from God and that Christians must therefore obey the established government. When Anastasio Somoza was killed in 1956 by the poet Rigoberto López, the bishops paid homage to the deceased by nominating him 'Prince of the Church'. One could multiply such examples.

The first signs of change came through a young Spanish missionary, Father José de la Jara, who had been influenced by the pioneering initiatives of a new pastoral community in the neighbouring country of Panama. This experience had been implemented at the parish of San Miguelito by an American priest, Father Leo Mahon from Chicago, a man who believed that the missionaries in Latin America should be 'revolutionaries, not "modernizers"'.[13]

With the help of Maryknoll sister Maura Clark – who was later killed in El Salvador in 1980 – and other sisters from various religious orders – Assumptionist, Theresian, Holy Heart of Jesus – José de la Jara in 1966 started the first 'base communities' at the parish of San Pablo, on the outskirts of Managua. Following the example of San Miguelito, he wanted to show that the parish was not above all a Church building or a territory, but a community of brothers and sisters, a 'Family of God'. The people, the laity, were to participate actively in Church life, by reading and discussing the Bible in a kind of 'Socratic dialogue' with the priest or lay celebrant. There was little political content in the curriculum [*cursillo*] of initiation, but the community gave its members – particularly the women – a feeling of personal dignity and collective initiative. The first result of this activity was the *Misa popular nicaragüense*, written and sung by the communities.

In 1968 some other parishes asked San Pablo for help in forming similar communities. Among them was the community of Solentiname, founded by Father Ernesto Cardenal. Father José de la Jara visited these new communities and suggested that they read and discuss the Gospel, as in Managua.

After the Medellín Conference there was a much broader development of the CEBs, which spread to several shantytowns in Managua and to the countryside, and with a growing radicalization. The religious orders – particularly the female ones – were very active in this process, receiving help from many foreign brothers and sisters, the most committed of whom were the Maryknolls, the Capuchins (who developed communities in the eastern and northern part of the country), the Jesuits and Assumptionists.

In 1969 the San Pablo community in Managua decided to create a Christian Youth Movement, which was to radicalize very quickly: in the early 1970s many of its members became activists or sympathizers of the Frente Sandinista de Liberación Nacional (FSLN). The Marxist guerrilla movement founded in the early 1960s by Carlos Fonseca and Tomás Borge eagerly received these young Christian radicals, without trying to impose any ideological conditions on them.

Meanwhile, at the Catholic University of Central America (UCA – Universidad Centro-Americana) two teachers – the Franciscan Uriel Molina and the Jesuit Fernando Cardenal (Vice-Rector of the UCA) – began a dialogue with the Marxist students linked to the FSLN. Some Christian students from the UCA decided in 1971 to live in the parish of Father Uriel Molina, the 'El Riguero' neighbourhood in Managua, and to share the community life of the poor. They formed the Christian University Movement, which soon established links with the FSLN while remaining independent. Finally, in 1973, priests (including Fernando Cardenal) and students from the UCA and from the *barrios* of East Managua formed the Christian Revolutionary Movement, several hundred members of which soon joined the Sandinistas. The first Christian cell of the FSLN was formed with the participation of Luis Carrión, Joaquín Cuadra, Álvaro Baltodano and Roberto Gutiérrez, who would all become important leaders in the Front.

In the countryside the Capuchins and Jesuits helped to create a lay leadership, the Delegates of the Word [Delegados de la Palabra], in order to celebrate certain sacraments in the rural areas not regularly served by a priest. They were trained to provide not only religious services but also literacy courses, health and agricultural information, and they organized community meetings around biblical texts, at which the problems of the community were debated. In order to educate the Delegates of the Word, the Jesuits created in 1969 the Evangelical Committee for Agrarian Advancement (Comité Evangélico de Promoción Agraria – CEPA), which was active in the areas of Carazo, Masaya, León, Estelí – future strongholds of the insurgency. This grass-roots activity of priests, religious and lay Catholics flourished outside the direct control of the bishops.

The theological and political radicalization of the Delegates of the Word, and their frequent victimization by Somoza's National Guard, led many of them to the ranks of the Sandinista movement. In 1977 several of these peasant leaders formed a rural union, the Association of Workers of the Countryside (Asociación de Trabajadores del Campo – ATC), which co-operated with the Sandinistas. By 1978, the CEPA had cut its formal links with the Church and became an independent Christian organization, also sympathetic to the FSLN.

Similar, although less radical, activities took place among the Protestants. After the 1972 earthquake Protestant leaders created an Evangelical Committee for Aid and Development (CEPAD), which engaged in human rights activities and became increasingly hostile to the Somoza regime. There were also several Protestant pastors who supported the Sandinistas.

In 1977, several young people from the Solentiname community of Ernesto Cardenal took part in an FSLN attack on the San Carlos barracks of the National Guard. In reprisal the Somoza Army destroyed the community and burnt it to the ground. The same year, a Spanish-born priest, Father García Laviana, a Missionary of the Sacred Heart who had arrived in Nicaragua in 1970, joined the FSLN. In a letter dated December 1977, he explained his decision by referring to the Medellín solution which said: 'Revolutionary insurrection may be legitimate in the case of a clear and persistent tyranny which gravely endangers fundamental human rights and greatly harms the common good of the nation, whether this tyranny originates in one individual or in clearly unjust structures.' In a second letter, in 1978, Father Laviana tried to explain the link between religious and socio-political motives in his action:

> My faith and my belonging to the Catholic Church oblige me to take an active part in the revolutionary process with the FSLN. For the liberation of an oppressed people is an integral part of Christ's total redemption. My active contribution in this process is a sign of Christian solidarity with the oppressed and those who struggle to free them.[14]

On 11 December 1978, he was killed in an encounter with the National Guard.

As the crisis of the regime deepened, the Church hierarchy became increasingly critical of Somoza. On 6 January 1978, the Nicaraguan Bishops' Conference issued a 'Message to the People of God':

> We cannot remain silent when the largest part of our population suffers inhuman living conditions as a result of a distribution of wealth that is unjust by any standard . . . when the death and disappearance of many citizens in city and country remains a mystery . . . when the citizens' right to choose their authorities is falsified in the game of political parties.[15]

A few days later Pedro Joaquín Chamorro, editor of *La Prensa*, and one of the main leaders of the liberal opposition, was assassinated: this was to be the beginning of the end for Somoza. Although opposed to the regime, the bishops refused to give any kind of support to the FSLN. Monsignor Obando y Bravo, the Archbishop of Managua, declared in his message of August 1978:

> Violence not only threatens to make more remote the possibility of building the Kingdom of God based on brotherhood and justice but also is self-defeating for those who would use it. . . . To think of

resolving our antagonisms once and for all by means of escalation, be it in the form of government repression or revolutionary insurrection, would only plunge our society into an abyss of blood and destruction with incalculable consequences for our social and spiritual life.[16]

No distinction is made in this statement between government repression and revolutionary insurrection – both are rejected in the name of non-violence.

However, a very large number of Christians, particularly young and poor people, ignored the Archbishop's advice, and actively took part in the insurrection – or rather, the series of local insurrections of 1978–79 which led up to the final uprising in Managua, the flight of Somoza and the victory of the Sandinistas on 19 July 1979. The areas where the struggle was most intensive, and the action best organized and effective, were precisely those where CEBs, Delegates of the Word and radical Christians had been active in the preceding years: Monimbo, Masaya, Chinandega, León, Matagalpa, Estelí, the eastern *barrios* of Managua, and Open Tres, a poor shantytown on the outskirts of the capital. Moreover, many priests, religious (particularly Capuchins and Jesuits) and nuns gave direct help to the Sandinistas, providing them with food, shelter, medicine and ammunition.

The historical novelty of this sort of massive Christian (both lay and clergy) participation in the revolution, as a decisive component of the process, was not lost on the Sandinista Front, which acknowledged in its Declaration on Religion of 7 October 1980 (published in *Barricada*, Managua):

> Christians have been an integral part of our revolutionary history to a degree unprecedented in any other revolutionary movement of Latin America and possibly the world. . . . Our experience has shown that it is possible to be a believer and a committed revolutionary at the same time, and that there is no irreconcilable contradiction between the two.

Of course, not all Christians supported the revolution. The Church was divided (after a short 'period of grace') between those who were, as one said in Nicaragua, *con el proceso* (with the revolutionary process unfolding after July 1979) and those who opposed it. While most bishops became increasingly hostile to Sandinismo, the great majority of the religious orders (in particular the Jesuits and Maryknolls) sided with the FSLN. The diocesan clergy was divided between the two options, with the greater number supporting the bishops.

The most visible figures of the pro-Sandinista Christian minority were, of course, the three priests who became ministers in the new government:

• Ernesto Cardenal: born in 1925, he was consecrated priest in 1965. As a follower of the famous American Catholic theologian Thomas Merton, he lived for two years (1957–58) at his Trappist Convent of Gethsemany in Kentucky. After his return to Nicaragua he founded the community of Solentiname in 1966. A well-known poet, Cardenal visited Cuba in the early 1970s and became increasingly radicalized. After the destruction of Solentiname he went into exile in Costa Rica and joined the FSLN (1977). In 1979 he became Minister of Culture.

• Fernando Cardenal, his brother: a Jesuit priest since 1968, he lived for one year among the poor in Medellín, Colombia (in 1969). In 1970 he was appointed Vice-Rector of the UCA in Managua by the Jesuit Order. Founder of the Revolutionary Christian Movement in 1973, he became a sympathizer of the Sandinistas. In 1979 he was appointed head of the Literacy Crusade, and in 1984 Minister of Education.

• Miguel d'Escoto: born in Hollywood, California, in 1933, he was educated in the USA, where he joined the Maryknoll Order. As a missionary in Santiago, Chile, he worked with the poor from 1963 to 1969. From 1970 to 1979 he lived in the USA as Director of Social Communications of the Maryknoll Society. From 1979 to 1990 he was Minister of Foreign Relations in the Nicaraguan government.

For some time another priest, Edgar Parrales, a Franciscan, was Minister of Social Welfare. Many other ministers and high-ranking officials of the revolutionary government were well-known lay Catholic figures: Roberto Argüello, Carlos Tünnerman, Reinaldo Téfel, Emilio Baltodano, María del Socorro Gutiérrez, Vidaluz Meneses, Francisco Lacayo, etc.

The Christians who were *con el proceso* organized themselves within several structures:

• The Antonio Valdivieso Ecumenical. Centre (including Catholics and Protestants), founded in August 1979 by Franciscan Father Uriel Molina and Baptist Minister José Miguel Torres. It organizes meetings, conferences, publications and research projects.

• The Central American University (UCA), run by the Jesuits.

- The Historical Institute for Central America (IHCA), led by the Jesuit Álvaro Argüello. In 1980 the Institute published a series of very radical pamphlets presenting a Christian revolutionary perspective, the *Folletos Populares Gaspar García Laviana*. It also publishes a widely respected monthly information bulletin, *Envío*.
- Although non-confessional, the journal *Pensamiento Proprio*, edited by Jesuit Xavier Gorrostiaga (of Basque origin), is also linked to the pro-Sandinista Christian tendency. It has an important role because of its competent and independent analysis of developments in Nicaragua and Central America.
- The Association of the Nicaraguan Clergy (ACLEN), also led by Álvaro Argüello. It was dissolved by the bishops in 1983.
- The most important of all: several hundred base communities, in the provinces and in Managua. Some of them are co-ordinated in local networks, such as the Inter-Community Bloc for Christian Welfare (BIBCS) in the north-eastern region (León-Chinandega). On the Atlantic Coast (where American Capuchin bishops are present) and in Estelí (which has a moderately progressive bishop) there was no tension between the hierarchy and the CEBs. But in Managua the base communities, which were active in the poor neighbourhoods and very politicized, were in open conflict with Cardinal Miguel Obando y Bravo.

This active Christian participation – which also includes many Protestants: in 1980, some five hundred ministers signed a statement offering to co-operate with the revolutionary process – deeply influenced Sandinismo itself, as an ideology composed of Sandino's radical agrarian nationalism, revolutionary Christianity and the *Guevarista* brand of Latin American Marxism. The language, symbols, images and culture of Sandinismo were often borrowed from the Gospel: this can be seen both at the grass roots of the movement and in the speeches of some of the main FSLN leaders, such as Luis Carrión and Tomás Borge. The practice of the Front was also influenced by Christian ethics: the Nicaraguan Revolution abolished capital punishment and became the first modern revolutionary movement since 1789 to consolidate its victory without executions, guillotine or firing squads.

At first, the bishops seemed to accept the revolution. Their statement of 17 November 1979 was astonishingly progressive: it favoured a socialism that would lead to a 'true transfer of power toward the popular classes', and aim to satisfy the needs of the majority of Nicaraguans through a nationally planned economy. Although it rejected 'class hatred', it accepted class struggle as 'the dynamic factor . . . leading to a just transformation of structures'. It called for radical social change, beyond 'the defence of individual interests, whether large or small'. And finally, it proclaimed: 'our faith in Jesus and in the God of life . . . should illuminate the commitment of Christians in the present revolutionary process'.[17]

However, after the liberal members of the coalition government (Alfonso Robelo and Violeta Chamorro) broke with the FSLN in April 1980, the bishops turned increasingly against the *proceso*. In May 1980 they called on the three priests to leave the government and, during the following years, engaged in open confrontation with the Sandinistas and radical Catholics. During his visit in 1983, the Pope naturally supported the bishops and denounced the 'People's Church', ordering the Cardenal brothers and Miguel d'Escoto to give up their governmental responsibilities. When they refused to comply, they were suspended or expelled from their religious orders (in 1984). In 1985 Monsignor Obando, having just been appointed Cardinal by Rome, travelled to Miami and expressed solidarity with the *contra* leaders. Soon several priests were accused of counter-revolutionary activity by the government and expelled from the country.

Committed Christians who sided with the revolutionary process tried at the same time to preserve their own specific identity, combining support with criticism of the Sandinista leadership. For instance, in a statement released in June 1985 ('Church and Revolution in Nicaragua') the Antonio Valdivieso Ecumenical Centre emphasized:

> We recognize the FSLN as the vanguard of the people. . . . However they can make mistakes, and in these difficult years of transition they have often made mistakes, even on very important issues like the Miskito problem, land reform, censorship of the press, etc. They have also made some mistakes, in our view, in relation to the Church: for instance, the expulsion of ten priests. . . . [But] we also see the honesty with which the leaders of the FSLN recognized and corrected some of these mistakes.[18]

It would be beyond the scope of the present chapter to discuss the various aspects of the relationship between religion and politics during the twelve years of the Sandinista experiment. The support of progressive Christians certainly helped the Sandinistas to win the elections of 1984, but it could not prevent their defeat six years later, under more difficult economic and political circumstances. It is hard to assess the importance of religious factors in the victory of the anti-FSLN coalition. Other aspects were probably more important (the economic situation, the popular rejection of military service) but it is obvious that the support given by the Church (particularly Monsignor. Obando) and by the new evangelical movements, to Violeta Chamorro, helped her to win the elections in 1990.

El Salvador: from Jesuit 'conscientization' to social rebellion

As in Nicaragua, it was only after the conference of Medellín that things began to change in the Salvadorean Church. Under the influence of the new orientation adopted in 1968 by the Latin American bishops and of the first writings of liberation theology – those, for instance, of Jon Sobrino, a Basque Jesuit living in El Salvador – a group of priests started missionary work among the poor peasants of the diocese of Aguilares in 1972–73. The central figure in this group was Father Rutilio Grande, a Salvadoran Jesuit who taught at the seminary of San Salvador, but decided to leave the city to share the life of the rural poor. The priests' missionary team (many of them Jesuits) lived among the peasants and initiated base communities, conceived by them as 'a community of brothers and sisters committed to building a new world, with neither oppressors nor oppressed, according to God's plan'. They read the Bible to the peasants and compared their lives to those of the Hebrews, who were slaves in Egypt under the Pharaoh, but liberated themselves through collective action. An average of seven hundred people attended weekly CEB meetings and their circle of influence ranged from two to five thousand.

The traditional religious structures of the villages, the so-called societies of 'Adorers of the Holy Sacrament' whose main activity was to say the rosary, were replaced by Delegates of the Word (as in Nicaragua, also on the initiative of the Jesuits), who read the Bible with the community. The missionaries attempted to break what they considered to be the passivity of traditional peasant religion, and told the believers that instead of just 'adoring' Jesus it was more important to follow his example and struggle against evil in the world, that is, against *social sin*, identified (by them) with exploitation and capitalism. They also promoted self-assurance among the peasants, generating the rise of a new leadership elected by the community.[19]

There is a glimpse of the explosive brand of political/religious *Brüderlichkeitsethik* (to use Weber's term) preached by Father Rutilio in the following passage from his last sermon in 1977: 'Our ideal is like the Eucharist, a large common table with room for all. In this country to preach the Gospel is subversive. If Jesus came to us again, they would call him a rebel, a subversive, a Jewish foreigner, a propagandist of exotic and foreign ideas. They would crucify him.'[20]

One month later he was shot by the Army.

The religious change brought political conversions (charged with religious feelings). The 'awakening through the Scriptures' led to militant action and 'conscientization' (consciousness-raising) led to organization. As traditional religion became revolutionary religion, it led to revolutionary politics. Some radical Christians began to be attracted by the revolutionary guerrilla movements, particularly the 'Farabundo Martí' People's Liberation Forces (FPL) a leftist split from the Communist Party.

One of the Delegates of the Word educated by Father Rutilio, Apolinario Serrano ('Polín'), became in 1974 the president of a new Christian peasant union (the Federación Cristiana de Campesinos del Salvador – FECCAS). Soon FECCAS converged with another peasant union (the Union de los Trabajadores del Campo – UTC), with the teachers' union (the Asociación Nacional de Educadores d'El Salvador – ANDES) and with students' and pupils' movements to found a common organization, the Revolutionary People's Bloc (Bloque Popular Revolucionario – BPR), which was sympathetic to the guerrilla movement. The main leader of the BPR was Juan Chacon, a young Christian activist and organizer of base communities.

The Church hierarchy was divided: while the archbishop, Monsignor Romero and the auxiliary bishop, Monsignor Rivera y Damas, denounced the military's repression of popular movements and the killing of priests and lay activists, the other three bishops supported the Army – one of them, Monsignor Álvarez, even had the title of Colonel in the Armed Forces. In September 1979, when the Army killed Apolinario Serrano and three other leaders of FECCAS, there was such popular outrage that one month later the dictatorship of General Romero was ousted by the armed forces themselves. A coalition government was formed, including moderate leftists such as the social-democrat Guillermo Ungo. But the military kept real power in their own hands and blocked any reform, while continuing the extra-judicial executions. Two months later, in December 1979, the progressive ministers withdrew from the coalition government and were replaced, a few months later by the Christian Democrats of Napoleon Duarte. Soon after, in March 1980, Monsignor Romero was killed by a death-squad (following orders from Major d'Aubuisson) while celebrating mass. During his funeral the Army again shot at the people, killing thirty-five.

In November 1980 all the leaders of the legal opposition, the Democratic Revolutionary Front (FDR), including Juan Chacon (the head of the BPR), were executed by the Army. And in December 1980, four North American women missionaries were raped and killed by the military: three nuns – Maura Clarke, Ita Ford (both of the Maryknoll Order) and Dorothy Kazel – and one lay missionary, Jean Donovan.

The response to all these killings began in January 1981, when the newly formed guerrilla coalition of five armed groups, the Farabundo Martí National Liberation Front (FMLN), launched a general offensive against the Army. It was the beginning of a civil war which raged for twelve years. The FMLN was the heir of two different traditions which converged during the 1970s: that of the rebel Christians and that of the dissident Marxists. The mass base for the insurgency in the rural areas came mainly from FECCAS, the Christian peasant union, and in the towns, to a large extent, from the CEBs. Unlike in Nicaragua, however, the result was to be not a fusion, or symbiotic relation, between religion and politics, but rather the absorption of the first by the second – even if the Christian component remained lively, particularly at the grass roots.

One of the unique features of the events in El Salvador is the eminent role played by a charismatic bishop who began as a conservative but became, according to Jean Donovan (the lay sister killed in 1980), 'the leader of liberation theology in practice': Monsignor Romero. His evolution during the years 1977–80 is an almost ideal-type example of the transformation of institutional religiosity into soteriological ethics of fraternity.

Born in 1917 into a humble family (his father was a telegraph operator), Oscar Romero became a priest in 1942 and studied theology in Rome (1943). In 1966, he became secretary of the

Salvadorean Conference of Bishops. In 1970 he was appointed auxiliary Bishop of San Salvador and in 1977 Archbishop of the capital. As he would later say to friends, he was chosen as the one most able to neutralize the 'Marxist priests' and CEBs and improve relations between the Church and the military government, which had deteriorated under the former bishop (Monsignor Chavez).

Indeed, Monsignor Romero initially appeared as a rather conservative bishop, both because of his past (he had sympathized with the Opus Dei in his youth) and because he believed in personal prayer and personal conversion rather than social change. He criticized the base communities for being too politicized and losing their Christian identity. He identified the glory of God with the glory of the Church and was very ecclesiastical, attached to the canons and discipline of the institution. He was considered by the radical priests as a 'purely spiritual' figure and a traditionalist.

His 'conversion' to a new ethical and socio-religious perspective began with the murder of Father Rutilio Grande in March 1977. Deeply shaken by the death of the Jesuit missionary, Monsignor Romero broke with the government of Colonel Molina and refused to take part in any official celebration as long as the murder had not been investigated. After another priest was killed (Alfonso Navarro, May 1977) and the Aguilares parish house destroyed by the military (with the arrest of four Jesuits and three hundred parish members), he became increasingly outspoken in his protest against violations of human rights by the military.

After 1978 Monsignor Romero became deeply influenced by the liberation theologian Jon Sobrino, who advised him on the writing of his pastoral letters. He entered into growing conflict with the conservative bishops, the papal Nuncio, the military, the oligarchy, and finally the Pope himself (during a visit to Rome). He had regular meetings with radical priests and the base communities, and later with trade unionists and BPR militants.

His Sunday sermons were attended by thousands in the Cathedral and followed by hundreds of thousands through the Church's radio station (ISAX). They linked the Bible and life of the Church with social and political events, from the standpoint of the poor. One of his leitmotivs was the self-emancipation of the poor – the central *topos* of liberation theology, as in this homily from 2 February 1980:

> The hope which our Church encourages is not naive, nor is it passive;
> it is rather a summons for the great majority of the people, the poor,

that they assume their proper responsibility, that they raise their consciousness, that in a country where it is legally or practically prohibited they set about organizing themselves. . . . Liberation will arrive only when the poor are the controllers of, and protagonists in, their own struggle and liberation.[21]

A few days later, Monsignor Romero published his letter to President Carter, requesting him not to provide military aid to the Salvadorean regime and not to interfere in the determination of the destiny of the Salvadorean people – a document which had an immediate international impact. He knew very well that his life was in danger; in an interview with the Mexican daily *Excelsior* he said:

I have often been threatened with death. . . . If I am killed, I will be resurrected in the Salvadorean people. . . . Martyrdom is a grace of God which I do not think that I deserve. But if God accepts the sacrifice of my life, let my blood be a seed of freedom and the sign that hope will soon become reality. One bishop may die, but the Church of God, which is the people, will never perish.[22]

Finally, in his sermon at the Metropolitan Cathedral on 23 March, Monsignor Romero dared to take an unprecedented step: he called on the soldiers not to obey their superiors:

I would like to make a special appeal to the members of the Army. . . . Brothers, each one of you is one of us. We are the same people. The peasants you kill are your own brothers and sisters. When you hear the voice of a man commanding you to kill, remember instead the voice of God: 'Thou Shalt not Kill!' God's law must prevail. No soldier is obliged to obey an order contrary to the law of God. There is still time for you to obey your own conscience, even in the face of a sinful command to kill. . . . In the name of God, in the name of our tormented people whose cries rise up to Heaven I beseech you, I beg you, I command you: STOP THE REPRESSION !

The next day he was killed by the paramilitary death-squads.[23]

Monsignor Romero's sacrifice made him into a charismatic symbol for committed Christians in Latin America and beyond – not unlike Camilo Torres in the 1960s, but this time as a non-violent prophet. His last years illustrate in a dramatic way not only the possibility of radical changes in the religious culture ('conversion') of members of the episcopal hierarchy – motivated less by abstract theological considerations than by the collision of pastoral concerns with institutional violence – but also the limits of a purely 'functional' or 'institutional' explanation of their behaviour.

After the death of Monsignor Romero, Monsignor Rivera y Damas became Archbishop of San Salvador. Although much more cautious and moderate than his predecessor, he still defended human rights against military violence. However, following his retreat in 1995, Rome nominated in his place a former bishop of the Army, Monsignor Fernando S. Lacalle, a conservative figure belonging to the Opus Dei.

It is beyond the scope of this section (dedicated to the religious roots of rebellion) to examine the various developments during the twelve years of civil war in El Salvador. As is well known, a compromise negotiated between the FMLN and the government brought the conflict to an end in 1993. But before that, in December 1990, Ignacio Ellacuría – a Jesuit of Spanish origin and rector of the UCA, one of the leading liberation theologists and an outspoken advocate of a negotiated solution for the war – as well as six other Jesuit professors of the Catholic University (and two women who worked for them) were killed by the Salvadorean Army. The international outrage provoked by this collective assassination was one of the reasons why the military were forced to agree to take part in negotiations.[24]

Liberationist and Conservative Protestantism

Liberationist Christianity is not only Catholic: as already mentioned, it also has a significant Protestant branch that developed in a parallel way during the 1960s and the 1970s, often associated, in various forms, with its Catholic counterpart. It is rooted in the religious culture of the so-called 'historical' Protestant denominations, such as Lutherans, Presbyterians, Methodists, Unitarians – as opposed to the more recent Pentecostal sort of evangelical Churches. It has a distinctly ecumenical spirit, not only neglecting the traditional Protestant battle against the Roman Church, but sharing common theological and pastoral initiatives with progressive Catholics.

According to one of the most important representatives of Protestant liberation theology, José Míguez Bonino, an Argentinian Methodist minister and lecturer at the Evangelical Institute of

Buenos Aires, the make-up of the progressive theologians of both Christian denominations has many resemblances but also some differences. Among the latter he mentions 'membership in a minority religious community with a tradition of avoiding explicit politics while maintaining de facto ties with the system of liberal capitalism and the "neocolonial" setup, and a theological tradition going back to the Reformation'. While he insists that the common situation and project take first place, with relative differences in the background, Míguez Bonino believes that Protestant theologians have certain responsibilities of their own. Considering the Protestant 'distinction of planes' served as an ideological justification for exempting the liberal, capitalist, bourgeois set-up from all prophetic criticism, liberation theology requires 'a radical and justified critique of the classic Protestant tradition': 'it is not simply a matter of adapting or reformulating. They must radically reconsider the whole theological perspective in which they have been brought up.'[25]

On the other hand there are some aspects of liberation theology that have an obvious Protestant background, even if they may also be found among Catholics: the frequent references to Old Testamentarian *loci*, the central importance of communitarian Bible-reading, the emphasis on the local community as against the ecclesiastic hierarchy. Not surprisingly, Protestant theologians have been among the most active promoters of a new interpretation of the biblical sources.

Two figures played a pioneering role in the rise of Protestant liberationist Christianity: Richard Shaull and Rubem Alves.

As an American Presbyterian missionary in Brazil (1952–64), Richard Shaull lectured at the Theological Seminary of Campinas (State of São Paulo) and worked with the UCEB, the (Protestant) Brazilian Union of Christian Students, which during the late 1950s underwent a similar process of radicalization as its Catholic rival, the JUC. In his book *Christianity and Social Revolution* (1960) Shaull called on the students to commit themselves to the struggle for a more just and egalitarian society ('as an alternative both to capitalism and to communism'), and in 1962 he helped to organize in Recife a conference of progressive Protestants (the Department for Social Responsibility of the Brazilian Evangelical Confederation) on 'Christ and the Brazilian revolutionary process'.[26]

As a result of his willingness to work in fraternal alliance with Marxists and with progressive Catholics (the Dominicans of São Paulo) Shaull came into growing conflict with the Presbyterian

Church, and was eventually forced to leave the country in 1964. However, he had already sowed new ideas among Protestant students and seminarists, who would later become leading figures of liberationist Christianity in Brazil and Latin America.

Among Shaull's students at the Seminary of Campinas was Rubem Alves, a lay theologian who continued his studies at Princeton, where he presented a doctoral thesis in 1968 with the prophetic title: *Towards a Theology of Liberation*. The expression – used here for the first time – seemed so strange to Alves's publishers that they rejected it: the book appeared in English as *A Theology of Human Hope* and in Spanish as *Christianity: Opium or Liberation?*

In a way, this book may be considered the first piece of liberation theology in Latin America, although it deals with general issues and hardly mentions Latin America. Mainly inspired by progressive European Protestant theology (Bultmann, Moltmann, Bonhoeffer), Alves calls for a political humanism, for a Christian consciousness committed to the historical liberation of human beings, and for a theology speaking the language of liberty, as a historical and radically prophetic language. He also denounces the condition of the Third World nations, which have been deprived of the freedom to plan their own future.[27]

Unlike his Catholic counterparts (Hugo Assmann, Gustavo Gutiérrez), Rubem Alves does not speak as a Brazilian or Latin American theologian, nor does he use such Marxist concepts as dependency, capitalism, or class struggle. Nevertheless, his pioneering work was a starting point for liberation theology and had a significant influence, particularly among the Protestant youth.

Perhaps the most important initiative in creating a liberationist movement among Latin American Protestants was the formation, in 1961, of ISAL, Iglesia y sociedad en América Latina (Church and Society in Latin America), at a meeting in Huampani, near Lima, Peru. Under the leadership of lay figures such as Luis E. Odell and Hiber Conteris, ISAL mobilized progressive believers of various Protestant denominations, in a permanent dialogue with leftist Catholics and Marxists. Through its activities and its journal, *Cristianismo y Sociedad*, it called for a Christian commitment to the popular movements and proposed a new interpretation of the Scriptures. Of course, for the majority of the Protestant Churches in Latin America such a radical stance was unacceptable: in spite of ISAL's attempt to keep up a dialogue with them, they gradually cut their links with it.

In 1967, at a conference which took place near Montevideo, ISAL decided to concentrate its efforts in programmes of popular education, using Paulo Freire's new pedagogy. Such a practice of popular conscientization led almost naturally to popular mobilization: in Bolivia, for instance, ISAL became one of the main forces in the struggle against military dictatorship and for popular organization. During the early 1970s ISAL leaders and activists were harshly repressed by the various military regimes which took over Latin America: some were killed, others were imprisoned, and many had to go into exile. ISAL ceased to function in 1975.[28]

Nevertheless, the liberationist current continued to exert a significant influence among the Protestant Churches – in particular through the CLAI (Council of Latin American Churches), a broad co-ordinating institution created at the Evangelical Conference of Oaxtepec (Mexico) in September 1978 by 110 Protestant Churches and 10 ecumenical organizations representing 19 Latin American countries. In his opening speech, Carmelo Álvarez, president of the Latin American Biblical Seminary of San José, Costa Rica, argued forcefully that 'a situation of domination, exploitation and dependency has characterized all levels of life in our continent'. In this situation, our 'history testifies to a church handed over to the dominant classes, but also shows the face of a church that opts for living from the "underside of history"'.

Some quite radical papers were presented at the conference, for instance by the study group on power structures: 'The doctrine of National Security provides the justification for the power exercised by the First World capitalists and the dominant social classes within each country. These power structures are ultimately the causes of . . . malnutrition, infant mortality, unemployment; short life spans; inadequate health care, lack of education and social security.' The Protestant Churches, according to this document, must reject Paul's charge in his Letter to the Romans regarding obedience to one's government. The Churches that co-operate with despotic regimes 'represent an alliance with and support of Pharaoh against Moses and the people of God who look for their liberation'.[29]

Of course, these radical theological views were far from being shared by all members of the CLAI, but for conservative evangelicals they were intolerable. In 1982, under the leadership of the preacher Luis Palau, they decided to break any links with CLAI and with all ecumenical Protestants related to the ('leftist') World Council of Churches, and to create a rival organization, CONELA (Latin American Evangelical Confederation).

Among the most important figures in Protestant liberation theology are some well-known biblicists, such as Milton Schwantes, Elsa Tamez and Jorge Pixley. They often work in co-operation with Catholics in ecumenical institutions such as the Ecumenical Department of Research (DEI) in Costa Rica, the Ecumenical Centre for Evangelization and Popular Education (CESEP) in São Paulo, or the Ecumenical Centre for Documentation and Information (CEDI) in Rio de Janeiro.

Jorge Pixley, a Baptist pastor and theologian living in Mexico, is probably the most gifted Protestant biblicist in Latin America. He published, together with the Catholic theologian Clodovis Boff one of the volumes of the key collection of books 'Theology and Liberation': *The Option for the Poor* (1986), which contains a very substantial section on the meaning of this choice in the Old and New Testaments.

In another book, *Exodus: An Evangelical and Popular Reading* (1983), Pixley explains the specific nature of the Protestant liberationist approach:

> This reading of the book of Exodus wants to be *evangelical* in the current meaning that we, of the evangelical or non-Roman Catholic Churches give to this word. These Churches, which derive in different ways from the Protestant Reformation in sixteenth-century Europe, believe that they find in the Bible the highest authority for their faith and they reject any ecclesiastic or scientific authority as a necessary mediation. This does not mean that one must reject ecclesiastic structures or scientific investigations. Simply, these sometimes useful mediations are not considered as always necessary.

Immediately afterwards he insists on the ecumenical and popular nature of his work:

> However, in its most important meaning, this commentary wants to be evangelical because it believes that, beyond our diverse denominational traditions, God has good tidings for the people. . . . In this sense, our evangelical reading goes beyond the limits of the non-Catholic Churches and wants to serve the whole Latin American people . . . Exodus belongs to God's people and not to the hierarchies of the Churches or to the specialists of the Academia.[30]

As the split between CLAI and CONELA shows, Protestants are deeply divided in Latin America. This division coincides to some extent (although not entirely) with the distinction between the older Protestant denominations and the rapidly expanding new Pentecostal churches.

The remarkable growth of the Pentecostal evangelical churches in Latin America – an event often described by Catholic observers as 'the invasion of the Protestant sects' – is one of the most important religious phenomena of recent years on the continent. Its political implications are quite obvious: while the historical Protestant confessions linked to the World Council of Churches are often socially concerned and include significant sectors sympathetic to liberation theology (as we have seen above), many of the so-called 'sects' – that is the evangelical and/or Pentecostal Churches – represent a fundamentalist and conservative religious culture which is either 'apolitical' (whatever that may mean) or downright counter-revolutionary.

The extent of the phenomenon is undeniable: a Brazilian bishop, Monsignor Bonaventura Kloppenburg, warned at the 1984 Conference of Latin American Bishops in Bogotá, that Latin America is turning Protestant faster than Central Europe did in the sixteenth century. Estimates are extremely difficult, because of the lack of reliable figures, but it seems that non-Catholic Christians now make up 10 per cent of the Latin American population; moreover, Protestants claim as much as 18 per cent of the population in Brazil, and some 25 per cent in Chile and Guatemala. In the last, the Protestant proportion of the population is supposed to have increased by nearly seven times. The vast majority of these Protestant believers (perhaps some three-quarters) are evangelical and/or Pentecostal. Of course, all these figures are questionable, both because of the tendency of evangelical missionary bodies to inflate their numbers, and because of the 'revolving door' quality of many congregations, whose members move easily from one church (or confession) to another.[31]

Evangelical or Pentecostal Churches – such as the Assemblies of God, the Church of God, the Word Church, etc – distinguish themselves from the traditional Protestant ones by their fundamentalism (a so-called 'literal' reading of the Bible), by their almost exclusive insistence on personal salvation (the 'born-again' individual), by magic practices such as 'faith healing', and by the intensive use of the most modern mass media ('tele-evangelism').

Evangelicals are not politically homogeneous; from this standpoint they can be represented (according to the useful image proposed by David Stoll), as a series of concentric circles: at the core, Churches or missionary agencies belonging to the religious Right, usually linked to some US institution (e.g. Pat Robertson's Christian Broadcasting Network) and often actively committed to US policy in Latin America (for instance the *contra* war in Nicaragua). The other concentric circles are also conservative, but as they move away from the core they become less and less explicitly political; in the last circle only can one find groups likely to oppose the religious Right, such as the Mennonites.[32]

The dominant conservative political/religious culture of most evangelical Churches often turns them into passive or ardent supporters of the status quo, and sometimes even of sinister military dictatorships, like those of Brazil, Chile and Guatemala. In north-eastern Brazil, in 1974, Assembly of God leaders encouraged their members to vote for the candidates of the military regime; and in Chile, one year after the bloody military coup of General Pinochet against the democratically elected government of Salvador Allende (1973), the leaders of thirty-two mainly Pentecostal Churches declared that this act had been 'God's answer to the prayers of all the believers who recognized that Marxism was the expression of a satanic power of darkness. . . . We the evangelicals . . . recognize as the highest authority of our country the military junta, who in answer to our prayers freed us from Marxism.'[33]

Many Latin Americans, particularly leftists and progressive Catholics, consider the 'invasion of the Protestant sects' as a US-promoted conspiracy against liberation theology, and more generally against all social movements for the emancipation of the poor. In fact, there are quite a few US evangelical missions whose behaviour largely corresponds with this (obviously one-sided) picture, in so far as they crudely identify their religious intervention in Latin America with the interests of US foreign policy. Considering the USA as a bastion of godliness and a missionary nation, some evangelicals were ready to place themselves at the service of the Reagan administration's geopolitical aims in Central America. The most obvious example is the notorious participation of evangelicals in the efforts of Colonel Oliver North to organize political and military support for the *contras* in the Nicaraguan civil war.

After the US Congress's decision to suspend aid to the *contras* – given their poor record in terms of human rights (destruction of clinics and schools, murder of civilians, rape of women, etc)

– Colonel North began recruiting 'anti-communist' evangelicals (with the blessing of the White House) into a 'private support network' for the Nicaraguan counter-revolutionary forces. Among the enthusiastic participants in this campaign, providing funding as well as political/religious support to the *contras* one can find: Pat Robertson's Christian Broadcasting Network, which organized an 'Operation Blessing', spending some two million dollars a year (the well-known tele-evangelist went personally to Honduras to review *contra* troops); Friends of the Americas, which received a humanitarian award from President Reagan in 1985; the Gospel Crusade, the Christian Emergency Relief Team, Trans World Missions, and other groups of the religious Right, most of them invited, co-ordinated and briefed by Colonel North.[34]

One cannot exclude the possibility that men like Oliver North are orchestrating evangelism elsewhere: some groups in Central America seem to have working relations with US embassies, through mechanisms such as USAID funding for private voluntary associations.[35] But this pattern has more relevance for Central America than for the countries of the Southern Cone, such as Brazil or Ecuador.

In any case, this 'conspiracy theory' is largely insufficient; above all, it does not explain why evangelical Protestantism has been so successful in winning a substantial popular following in several Latin American countries. Of course, one could argue that US dollars, massively invested by evangelical missionary agencies, were the means that ensured such remarkable results. This argument is far from being irrelevant: many wealthy US evangelical institutions practise so-called 'rice-bowl Christianity' and try to buy the loyalty of the poor by providing huge fundings for charity, development projects, church building, disaster relief, etc. By their superior financial power, evangelical agencies like World Vision are able to disrupt the patient work of grass-roots organizing linked to Catholic base communities. Trying to explain the substantial impact of World Vision among Quechua indigenous communities in Ecuador, Ana Maria Guacho, leader of the Indian Movement of Chimborazo (founded with the support of Monsignor Proaño, the 'Bishop of the Indians', who is known for his progressive commitment) argued: 'Organizing people isn't easy, when World Vision offers money and we offer consciousness-raising.'[36]

However, these kinds of explanation are too partial and one-sided to provide a true picture of the evangelical growth in Latin

America, which is too vast and complex a phenomenon to be understood only in terms of a US-funded missionary 'invasion' (which does of course exist). In fact, since the 1980s, Latin American evangelical Churches have become increasingly autonomous in relation to US Protestantism – even in Central America; by recruiting among the middle classes and the elites, evangelicals have been able to build their own local financial base. And in many countries, notably in the Southern Cone, new local evangelical Churches appeared, with their own 'prophets' and gurus, and with no links whatsoever to the main American denominations.

There is no single or simple explanation of this phenomenon: several social, political, cultural and (of course) religious aspects have to be taken into consideration (alongside those already mentioned), in order to give an account of the incredible expansion of the evangelical and Pentecostal Churches in many key countries south of the Rio Grande.

One important factor that certainly plays a role in the surprising rate of conversions in countries such as Guatemala and El Salvador is the fact that evangelical Churches have become a haven from government violence. The unambiguous commitment of many Catholic base communities, sisters, religious orders and even bishops to the struggles of the poor in these two countries has brought brutal and massive retaliations from the Army and para-military forces (death-squads) against the Catholic Church and its members: to be a Catholic in some areas of Central America is almost as dangerous as being considered a sympathizer with the revolutionary guerrillas. It is in this context that many individuals and even whole communities have joined evangelical Churches, known to be 'apolitical' and/or supportive of the military and their counter-insurgency policies (which, of course, is not considered by the authorities as being 'political'). In this case evangelical Protestantism has become a survival strategy for threatened people trying to protect themselves against State violence.

While in some cases this was basically a 'utilitarian' move, in others it corresponded to a feeling of defeat – particularly in Guatemala, where the revolutionary movement suffered many set-backs during the 1980s – and to changes in popular consciousness. More generally, one can say that conservative evangelicals appeal to a certain traditional popular culture of resignation, fatalism and acceptance of the given order of things – a tradition against which liberation theology has tried to fight in its 'consciousness-raising' grass-root activities. After a severe defeat, and confronted with military terror, the old feeling that 'things will never change' may once again become dominant in significant sectors of the population, some of whom move away from the Catholic Church and are attracted to the evangelical proposition of personal improvement by 'surrendering to Christ' – and to the safety of Churches considered respectable and holy by the ruling authorities.[37]

The appeal of personal improvement is in itself a powerful motive in conversions to evangelism. There is no doubt that a certain kind of puritan ethics can have concrete consequences in the daily life of poor families: by suppressing drinking, drugs, gambling and intercourse with prostitutes, 'born-again ' male individuals may significantly improve their economic condition, their health and their relations with wife and children. Little wonder that many poor women are active promoters of evangelical conversions, which hold the promise of a change in the erratic behaviour of their partners.

At the same time, by advising Latin Americans to concentrate on improving themselves by new moral conduct, instead of working for structural change, evangelical Churches discourage collective action and promote individual strategies of upward mobility. This sort of 'Protestant ethics' has without doubt a strong affinity with the 'capitalist spirit' of individual competition and private accumulation. According to the Argentinian preacher Luis Palau, one of the most important figures in Latin American evangelism, 'if we could eliminate infidelity and immorality in Latin America, we could cut poverty by half in one generation. . . . The vast middle class now emerging in Latin American Protestantism was converted poor and rose through industry, honesty and justice to the educated, reasonable life-style that is commonly called middle-class. I think that's the biblical anwer.'[38]

How far is the Weberian thesis relevant to Latin American Protestantism? In fact, evangelicalism can favour the adoption of a capitalist ethos of individual self-promotion – and therefore encourage the support of political forces committed to such an ethos. Chilean sociologist Claudio Veliz suggests in his recent book *The New World of the Gothic Fox* that the conversions have some similarities to a 'cargo cult': by adhering to evangelical Protestantism, people join a religion which seems to be closely bound up with the culture of industrial capitalism, a culture able to bring a prosperous good life, 'as well as to generate attractive consumer goods and cultural artefacts'.[39] However, to expect that this form of religion will by itself encourage capitalist development in Latin America is wishful thinking based on a misreading of Weber himself, who never argued that Calvinism 'caused' the rise of capitalism, but only pointed to the 'elective affinity' between the two.[40] The vast majority of the poor who convert to Pentecostalist denominations have few possibilities of upward mobility, and even fewer chances of becoming capitalists in the debt-ridden and depressed Latin American economies, where wealth is securely monopolized by a small elite. In any case, nobody has been able to find, so far, any particular manifestation of capitalist advance in the areas of greater evangelical influence.[41]

Several observers have noticed that uprooted populations expelled from their traditional settings, either by economic factors (agro-industrialization) or by counter-insurgency, are particularly receptive to evangelical proselytism. The safety-net of the small Church communities, based on strong emotional links, is certainly one of the reasons for the attraction of Pentecostalism – the more so if no Catholic base communities are available in the area.

Most of the reasons for the spectacular rise of evangelicalism in Latin America mentioned so far are more or less 'rational' if not utilitarian. There exists, however, an irreducible non-rational kernel in many of the conversions, which has to do with such magic rituals as faith healing, miracles and exorcisms, abundantly practised by most Pentecostalist sects. In this aspect, evangelical Protestantism, unlike historical Protestantism, is not a force of modernization, but rather a redeployment of popular Latin American religion. According to the sociologist Luis Samandu:

Pentecostal beliefs make possible the free expression of the popular religious world inhabited by demons, spirits, revelations and divine cures ... in such a way that believers recognize in Pentecostalism 'their' religion with profound roots in popular culture, long discredited as superstition by the cultivated and educated classes.[42]

Of course, the impossibility of access by the poor to modern medical facilities gives rise to the desperate attempt to find solace in miraculous healings. In more general terms, the catastrophes of modernity in Latin American urban centres are a favourable climate for the flourishing of magic beliefs: 'This is why the social disruption caused by capitalist development can be counted upon to multiply evil spirits, and why the march of "progress" over the last several centuries has, if anything, increased the demand for exorcism.'[43]

As we have seen, most of the evangelical denominations are either 'apolitical' – a term that in fact describes a stance supportive of the status quo – or extremely conservative. The country where they have had their most spectacular growth is also the one where, for a time, neo-Pentecostalists directly shared in the exercise of political power: Guatemala. The study of this case is an interesting – although extreme – illustration of 'evangelical politics'.

The growth of Pentecostalism in Guatemala during the 1970s runs parallel to the increasingly anti-leftist and anti-Catholic repression by the military, who considered all nuns, priests, religious orders, base community members and lay organizers as 'subversives' and guerrilla supporters. The assassinations of Catholics by military and paramilitary forces became so extensive that by 1980 the bishop of El Quiché (one of the main areas of conflict) took the unprecedented decision to withdraw from the diocese with all priests and sisters. Amnesty International issued a document in January 1981 under the heading 'A Government Programme of Political Murder'.[44]

After the 1976 earthquake, US evangelical Churches began to play a prominent role in the country: 'The assistance approach developed during the time of a natural catastrophe allowed some Protestant groups to control vast quantities of money and material resources . . . and to mobilize Protestant popular religion for the ruling interests of the military and the groups benefiting from control and stability'.[45] Intimate links began to develop between the Army and the Pentecostals, who shared anti-communism and anti-Catholicism: for instance, only they (and their NGOs) were allowed into the 'strategic villages' where the military regrouped indigenous communities from areas of conflict. Forcefully expelled from their lands, torn from their historical and cultural background, terrorized by the military, these populations become vulnerable to the evangelicals' aggressive campaigns of proselytism.[46] Clifford Kraus, correspondent for the *Wall Street Journal*, summed up the situation very accurately: 'Evangelical Christianity became a principal element of counterinsurgency – with the army helping to build churches for survivors.'[47]

A new degree of fraternity between the Guatemalan Army and evangelicals was attained when General Ríos Montt, a 'born-again' member of the Word Church, came to power through a military coup in March 1982. The Word Church was the Guatemalan branch of a Californian ministry, Gospel Outreach, which had arrived in the country in the wake of the 1976 earthquake. Its first recruits came from the upper classes, where many were strongly dissatisfied with the social and political choices of the Catholic Church, and were looking for some new denomination.

Ríos Montt explained to the people that he came to the presidency 'not through bullets, boots or ballots' but thanks to the Lord himself; in his frequent public preachings and sermons, he celebrated Guatemala as having now become the New Jerusalem of the Americas: 'Thank you, brothers, for telling the world: Guatemala is for Christ; thank you, brothers, for telling the world that here it is the Lord of Lords who commands.' In a faithful echo, the pastors of the Word Church explained to their flock: 'Today there exist in the world only two Christian governments: those of the United States and of Guatemala. It is not for believers to interfere with the business of justice or to change the established order. All this is the task of the government; and thank God, the government is in the hands of God.'[48]

In fact, military atrocities became even worse under Ríos Montt (March 1982–August 1983) than during the previous years: entire villages were wiped out, and thousands of men, women and children were killed in terrible massacres. According to a report by the Guatemalan Commission for Human Rights (CDHG), 14,934 people were killed in collective extra-judicial executions between 1981 and 1985, of whom 78 per cent died in 1982. The survivors were taken into care by evangelical aid foundations directly linked to the military and to Ríos Montt, under the co-ordination of such figures as Harris Whitbeck, a US missionary adviser to the Word Church and at the same time an engineer specializing in military constructions and counter-insurgency techniques, who acted as Ríos Montt's personal representative. Contributions from the USA were promoted by Pat Robertson, Bill Bright of the Campus Crusade for Christ and Jerry Falwell of the Moral Majority, and organized by Gospel Outreach under the suggestive name 'International Love Lift'.[49]

The elders of the Word Church acted as advisers to Ríos Montt, and helped to provide moral and religious legitimation for his policies. When confronted with evidence about the killings of whole Indian communities, they would either reject it as a 'smear campaign' or justify it by the need to root out 'subversion'. For instance, according to Word Church elder Francisco Bianchi, Ríos Montt's press secretary:

> The guerrillas won many Indian collaborators. Therefore the Indians were subversives. And how do you fight subversion? Clearly you had to kill Indians because they were collaborating with subversion. And then it would be said that you were killing innocent people. But they weren't innocent. They had sold out to subversion.[50]

An international outcry against the massive human rights violations and the theocratic leanings of the 'born-again' dictator made Ríos Montt into a burden for the ruling elite in Guatemala: in August 1983 he was finally ousted from the presidency by the military themselves. Admittedly, this is an exceptional case, but it reveals the kind of politics that some evangelicals are willing to implement, given the opportunity.

On the other hand, it should be stressed that a progressive minority has also existed among evangelicals, which has to be taken into consideration. For instance, there have been attempts to develop a moderately progressive theological and pastoral orientation – a sort of 'third way', distinct from both conservative fundamentalism and liberation theology – among some evangelical insitutions, such as the Latin American Theological Fraternity (Orlando Costas of Puerto Rico and René Padilla of Ecuador). Against fundamentalism, they called for 'contextualization', that is, an approach to the Bible going beyond the literalism of US evangelists, and trying to interpret Scripture in the Latin American context. Another, perhaps more radical, attempt took place at the Latin American Biblical Seminary in San José, Costa Rica, which became, according to conservatives, a hotbed of liberation theology during the late 1970s. When the seminary refused to implement a purge, the evangelical Latin American Mission withdrew its endorsement and twenty-five pastors linked to the proscribed institution were forced out of the Association of Costa Rican Bible Churches.[51]

There are also some interesting examples of active evangelical commitment to progressive social movements. One of the best known is the Nicaraguan Evangelical Committee for Aid to Development (CEPAD), which helped the FSLN during the insurrection of 1978–79. In October 1979, after the triumph of the Sandinistas, CEPAD sponsored a meeting of five hundred pastors pledging support for the revolutionary process.

But a more important case is Brazil, which nowadays has the second largest evangelical community in the world (after the USA). At the beginning of the 1960s some Brazilian Pentecostalists already actively participated – but without the support of their Churches – in the development of the Peasant Leagues, led by socialist lawyer Francisco Juliâo, and the Peasant Unions, led by former Pentecostal pastor Manuel da Conceição. In a retrospective comment, Francisco Julião observed that the evangelicals, always quoting from the prophet Isaiah, were among the most radical activists in the Leagues.[52] And more recently, several Pentecostalists joined the PT (Partido dos Trabalhadores – Workers' Party), including such well-known figures as Benedita da Silva, a black woman from a shantytown who, in 1993, became the party's candidate for the governorship of Rio de Janeiro and almost won.

Although most of the Brazilian evangelicals voted for the conservative/populist candidate Collor de Melo in the 1989 presidential elections, an evangelical movement in support of Lula, the PT candidate, came into being, under the leadership of Robinson Cavalcanti. One year later, Cavalcanti helped to found a Progressive Evangelical Movement, described by one of its leaders, Paul Freston, in the following terms: 'We call it "Movement" because it is an informal and supra-partisan association. "Evangelical" because it is conservative and orthodox in theology, reaffirming biblical authority and the importance of evangelization, conversion and prayer. And "Progressive" because it is committed to social change.'[53]

Brazilian progressive evangelicals refuse to be identified with liberation theology and leftist Catholicism: uninterested in ecumenism, they develop their own evangelical theology, 'integral Christianity', based on a strict biblical view of the world and of human beings. Their influence is hard to assess, but they seem to have a growing audience, not unrelated to the crisis provoked by several scandals of corruption involving leading conservative evangelical parliamentarians. In 1994 they once again called on evangelicals to vote for Lula, while asking the workers' candidate to take into account the Pentecostals' (rather conservative) positions against homosexuality and abortion, and for religious education in public schools.[54]

What is the likely political future of Latin American evangelism? Is it possible, as Cartaxo Rolim suggested in relation to Brazilian Pentecostalism, that through certains forms of social practice an understanding of social contradictions will arise among the

121

believers? Or that the social constituency of the evangelicals –
mainly the poor layers of the population – will sooner or later
force them to confront social change? Although he considers the
future of evangelical Protestantism in Latin America to be an
open-ended proposition, David Stoll concludes his study with a
sober assessment: the most probable scenario is that they will 'fail
to be a major force for social change'.[55]

Conclusion: Is Liberation Theology Finished?

Confronted with the Vatican's conservative counter-offensive, the extraordinary growth of the evangelical Churches, and the 'end of socialism' in Eastern Europe, is liberation theology finished? Has it become an episode of the past? Has it lost all social and cultural significance? According to many observers, scholars, sociologists, and newsmen the answer is yes. How far are these death notices justified?

There is no doubt that liberationist Christianity was affected by the spectacular success of the conservative brand of evangelicals among the Latin American poor. In some places, such as Guatemala, they were able to convert many former base community members, while in other countries the main impact of the new Churches seems to have been among the non-organized social layers, and in areas where the base communities were absent. Although there are some exceptions, it seems that the evangelicals have been able to grow mainly in the traditional Catholic parishes, whose lack of flexibility and poor communitarian life made them vulnerable to the new competitors in the 'religious market'. In any case, this growth raises a serious challenge to the attempt of liberationists – either Catholics or Protestants – to promote a culture of popular emancipation, in so far as an important part of their constituency seems to be choosing a traditionalist and non-committed form of religion.

It is also true that the new international and Latin American political context has not been favourable to radical Christians. The demise of the so-called 'really existing socialism' in the USSR and Eastern Europe generated a serious crisis among the Latin American Left. It did not affect the partisans of liberation theology as much as certain currents of the Left whose political and ideological identity was entirely dependent upon the Soviet model: their basic commitment being to the poor, rather than to any system of States, they were less disorientated and less vulnerable than many other progressives. However, the electoral defeat of the FSLN in the Nicaraguan elections of 1990 was a terrible blow, because the Sandinista Revolution had become a powerful inspiring example for a whole generation of Christian activists.

Considering these difficulties, and, above all, the Vatican's systematic hostility (on which more will be said later), could one not draw the conclusion, as has often been done, especially since 1989–90, that liberation theology is doomed to disappear – or has already lost its popular support?

While the decline of the movement is a distinct possibility, the prognosis of decease is, to say the least, too hasty. As the political scientist Daniel Levine, one of the best US specialists on religion and politics in Latin America recently argued:

> Notices of the death of liberation theology abound. . . . Such obituaries are premature. They misread the current situation, and reflect a basic misunderstanding of what liberation theology was and is all about. Liberation theology itself is depicted in static terms, and its 'success or failure' is tied closely to the short-term fortunes of movements or regimes. But liberation theology is anything but static: both the ideas and their expression in groups and movements have evolved substantially over the years. In any event, it is a mistake to confuse liberation theology with liberation itself. This distorts the real meaning of religious and political change in Latin America, and makes it hard to grasp the legacy they are likely to leave.[1]

The first evidence that one can observe is that, as a cultural movement and as a body of committed thinkers, liberation theology is alive and well. None of the important Latin American theologians has recanted from his former views or accepted the Roman criticism of them. Leonardo Boff has left his religious order and returned to the lay state but has done so in order to have greater freedom of expression and to continue his struggle in better conditions. There are, of course, significant differences between the various theologians – in particular, as we have seen above, between those who consider it important to fight for democracy in the Church (the Boff brothers) and those who leave aside internal ecclesiastic problems in order to concentrate on social action (Gustavo Gutiérrez) – but they all still share a basic commitment to the struggle of the poor for self-emancipation.

It is true that there has been an evolution, and that new issues and problems, new ways of approaching the social and religious reality in the continent, have appeared in their writings. For instance, many of them pay much greater attention to spirituality and popular religion. The concept of the poor has been extended, including not only the victims of the economic system, but also those oppressed because of their culture or ethnic origin – Indians and blacks. The special plight of women, doubly oppressed in patriarchal Latin American societies, has increasingly been taken into account.

While some tend to de-emphasize Marxism, or reduce it to one among many forms of social science, others – like Hugo Assmann, Enrique Dussel, Franz Hinkelammert, Pablo Richard, Jung Mo Sung – have developed, as we saw above, a new relationship to Marxism, by using the theory of commodity fetishism in their critique of capitalism as a false religion. This struggle against the idolatry of the market, conceived by liberation theology as a 'war of gods' between the Christian God of Life and the New Idols of Death, is the most radical and systematic expression so far of the Catholic anti-capitalist ethos.[2]

However, the key question is not the continuity of liberation theology as an intellectual movement, but its popular following. How far does it still have a broad influence, and to what extent does liberationist Christianity still exist as a social movement able to mobilize significant sections of the population?

It is hard to give a general answer. But there are some important events in Latin America which seem to indicate that the fire is far from being extinguished.

For instance, in 1990, a partisan of liberation theology, Father Jean-Bertrand Aristide, was elected President of Haiti: an unprecedented success for a socially committed religious leader. In fact, not only in Haiti, but also in other Latin American countries, important social and political upheavals of the 1990s – such as the indigenous rebellion in Chiapas – have been related, in one way ore another, to liberationist Christianity. The least that can be said is that these unexpected events do not quite fit with the predictions of its quick demise. Let us briefly examine these experiences.

Like most Latin American countries Haiti is predominantly Catholic, even if many believers also take part in voodoo (the Afro-Haitian religion) rituals, and in spite of the recent growth of evangelical Churches. While most of the Haitian bishops supported the dictatorship of the Duvalier dynasty (and the military rulers who succeeded it in power), a young Salesian priest started to organize popular resistance during the 1980s. Born in 1953 and educated at the Salesian seminary (where he discovered the writings of Leonardo Boff), Jean Bertrand-Aristide was sent by his superiors to study in Jerusalem and Montreal. After his return to Haiti in 1985 he soon became one of the main leaders of the *ti kominote l'egliz* – creole for Christian base communities. Quoting the Bible, he preached in his Church of St Jean Bosco in Port-au-Prince (Haiti's capital) against the Duvalier regime and its *Tontons macoutes* (paramilitary gangs), denouncing also the privileges of the rich oligarchy, the corruption of the State and the social injustice of the economic system. Accused of being a 'communist', he denied any Marxist inspiration, but insisted that he used Marx's writings as a tool among others, a tool that it would be senseless to ignore.

In 1986 Jean-Claude Duvalier was overthrown, but soon a military leader, General Namphy, took his place. Aristide and his young followers were among the main opponents of the new dictatorship, which was confronted with a growing popular resistance. Commenting some years later on his action, Jean-Bertrand Aristide said: 'I acted as a theologian in order to guide a political struggle: the irruption of the poor on the social scene.'[3]

The rebel priest escaped several attempts on his life, and his church was burnt down in September 1988, but he did not cease to preach against the military and the *Tontons*. Rome tried to send him to Canada but had to give up because of the militant opposition of the *ti l'egliz*. Finally, having considered that Father Aristide was guilty of 'incitement to hatred and violence, as well as of exalting class struggle', and that he had 'destabilized the community of the faithful', the Salesian Order decided to expel him in December 1988. Answering the accusations, Aristide wrote:

> I did not invent class struggle. Neither did Karl Marx. I would have preferred never to meet it. This may be possible if one never leaves the Vatican or the heights of Pétionville [a chic Haitian suburb]. In the streets of Port-au-Prince, who has not met class struggle? It is not a topic for controversy, but a fact, based on empirical evidence.[4]

In 1990 the authoritarian regime, threatened by the popular discontent and under international pressure, was forced to call elections. A broad popular coalition, Lavalas (Avalanche), composed of peasant associations, Christian base communities, youth movements and neighbourhood committees presented Aristide as the candidate of radical opposition to the ruling elite.

Combining the characteristics of political and religious charismatic leadership, Aristide was immensely popular; he nevertheless insisted, during his campaign, that he was no Messiah and could operate no miracles: 'The people should not put their trust in miracles. . . . The only miracle is for the people to become conscious of their strength and to take their fate into their own hands. They have to take away from the privileged ones what they want to keep only for themselves.'[5] On 16 December 1990, in the first democratic elections in the history of modern Haiti, Jean-Bertrand Aristide was elected President: in the first round he won 67 per cent of the vote, ahead of ten other candidates, including Marc Bazin, a US-supported 'demo-Christian' technocrat, who got only 14 per cent of the vote. Popular sympathy for Aristide was so strong that many pastors of the evangelical Churches, at a meeting before the elections, decided to withdraw support for the Protestant candidate, the pastor Silvio Claude, in favour of the radical young priest.

This election was a totally unprecedented event, not only in Haiti, but on the whole continent: never before in Latin America had a radical activist, with obvious leftist leanings, won such a sweeping electoral victory, and never before had a religious figure identified with liberation theology become the main leader of a popular movement.

In September 1991 President Aristide was overthrown by a military coup and forced into exile. Most of the bishops – with the exception of Monsignor Romelus, Bishop of Jérémie – and the papal nuncio supported the military. In fact, the Vatican was the only state that granted prompt diplomatic recognition to the *de facto* authorities. During the following three years of dictatorship, a brutal repression fell upon all popular movements and democratic forces. Thousands of Haitians were arrested, beaten, tortured or killed, and among them many Christians, lay or clerical, members of *ti l'egliz*, of Justice and Peace Commissions, or of the Caritas association (a bastion of progressive Catholics in Haiti). One of the best known of those was Father Jean-Marie Vincent, from the Order of the Montfortians: founder of the peasant movement *Têtes-Ensemble* (Heads Together), and for several years director of Caritas in the town of Cap Haitien, he called for the return of Aristide and became a leading figure of the popular opposition to the dictatorship. He was assassinated by the *Tontons macoutes* on 28 August 1994.

After three years of an ineffective international economic blockade, a United Nations-backed American intervention reinstated Jean-Bertrand Aristide as legal president of Haiti. Using his (limited) power to consolidate democracy, Aristide managed to dissolve the Haitian Armed Forces, and the coalition he supported – under the leadership of the political organization Lavalas – won a decisive victory at the municipal and parliamentary elections of 1995. It is still an open-ended story and it is too early to draw up a balance sheet of the achievements and shortcomings of his government. But the events in Haiti showed that liberationist Christianity was far from having exhausted its potential for social protest.

Another unexpected event was the Zapatista upsurge in Chiapas, Mexico, in January 1994: an armed uprising of several thousand Indians, under the leadership of a hitherto unknown organization, the EZLN (Zapatista Army of National Liberation). The Zapatistas denounced the lack of democracy in Mexico, the systematic repression of the indigenous communities by the landowners, Army, police and local authorities, the neo-liberal agrarian measures (suppression of Article 27 of the Constitution), and the NAFTA agreement between the US and the Mexican government. Taken by surprise, the authorities tried military repression and bombed the insurgent areas, but, confronted with massive support for the Zapatistas among the indigenous communities of Chiapas, were forced to retreat and to negotiate with the rebels.

The Zapatistas were described by the media and the government as inspired by liberation theology and led by Jesuits, while Monsignor Samuel Ruiz, Bishop of San Cristóbal de las Casas (Chiapas), was accused of being 'God's guerrilla fighter'. Both denunciations were, of course, widely off the mark. What happened with the Church in Chiapas and how far is it linked to the uprising?

Monsignor Samuel Ruiz, who studied at the Gregorian University in Rome, arrived in Chiapas in 1965; after taking part in the Medellín Conference he became, for several years, the head of the Department of Missions of CELAM. Influenced by liberation theology, he published in 1975 *Teología Bíblica de la Liberación*, which celebrates Christ as a revolutionary prophet.[6] By patient work in pastoral education – with the help of Jesuits, Dominicans and female religious orders – he created in his diocese a vast network of 7,800 indigenous catechists and 2,600 base communities. The pastoral agents helped to raise consciousness among the indigenous population, and to organize them in order to struggle for their rights, in particular for the recovery of their ancient lands. Monsignor Ruiz supported the indigenous communities in their confrontation with the landowners, especially the rich cattle-ranchers of Chiapas, and he also took under his protection the numerous Guatemalan refugees who arrived in southern Mexico, fleeing the brutal military repression in their country.

This very concrete and practical option for the poor led to an increasing conflict with the Mexican authorities and with the cattle-ranchers' association of Chiapas, who accused the bishop of 'agitating the Indians'. During the Pope's visit to Mexico in 1993 a strong campaign was launched asking for the removal of the 'troublemaker'. Monsignor Ruiz tried to win the support of John Paul II by handing him a pastoral letter containing the complaints and demands of the indigenous people of his diocese. However, a few months later, in October 1993, the papal nuncio in Mexico, Monsignor Geronimo Prigione, summoned Monsignor Ruiz to Mexico City and ordered him to resign – probably following a request from the Mexican authorities. While Monsignor Ruiz appealed to Rome against this decision, the Zapatista revolt took place and the Mexican government, unable to suppress the movement, had to call on Monsignor Ruiz as a mediator to negotiate with the EZLN.

In answer to the accusations, Monsignor Ruiz insisted that the Church as such was not linked to the insurrection: if some of its members took part in the movement, they did so in personal terms. Explaining the events, he said in a public declaration: 'The truth is that the Indians were tired of government promises and considered that there was no other way but to take arms. They were pushed beyond the limits of their patience.'[7]

From the available data, it appears quite obvious that neither Monsignor Ruiz nor his Jesuit and religious agents were 'promoters' of the uprising. As in El Salvador, consciousness-raising and the impulsion for self-organization created a new political-religious culture among a significant part of the indigenous population. In a second stage, revolutionary cadres, probably of Marxist background, built on this new social and political consciousness and helped to organize several thousand Indians, with the support of their communities, into an armed force. The ideology of the EZLN is not religious and draws its main symbolic references from the Mayan culture. It is true, however, that the patient work in education and empowerment of the indigenous communities by Monsignor Ruiz and his catechists created a favourable environment for the rise of the Zapatista movement.

The same can be said about a less spectacular but equally important indigenous uprising, which took place in Ecuador in June 1994. For many years the progressive sector of the Church had helped to promote an autonomous movement among the Quechuas. The charismatic Monsignor Leonidas Proaño, Bishop of Riobamba (Chimborazo), became well known in Latin America as 'the Bishop of the Indians' because of his lifelong commitment to social justice and in support of the Ecuadorian Indian outcasts. With the help of 1,300 pastoral agents, including lay and clerical, local, national and international personnel, he built an impressive network of parishes, schools, medical teams, centres and institutes, and in 1982 created, together with a group of Quechua leaders, the Indian Movement of Chimborazo (MICH). Monsignor Proaño and his followers rejected the capitalist model of development as destructive of the indigenous culture and society, and tried to propose an alternative model, a sort of Indian communitarianism, based upon the Quechua peasant tradition. Their action helped Indian communities throughout the country to become conscious of their rights and to lay claim to them for the first time in centuries. This is how a broad association was created, the National Indian Confederation of Ecuador (CONAIE). After his death in 1988, Monsignor Proaño was replaced by a new bishop, Monsignor Victor Corral, who continued the pastoral action of his predecessor.

In June 1994 the Ecuadorian government issued a neo-liberal agrarian law, which offered strong guarantees to private property and excluded any further distribution of land; it also aimed at the complete submission of agriculture to the exclusive logic of the market: the communitarian lands could be parcelled out and sold, and even water could be privatized. Criticizing the law, Monsignor Victor Corral declared: 'It only defends the interests and the viewpoint of the landowners who want to transform the country into an agro-industrial enterprise and reduce land to a commodity.'

The Indian movement – the CONAIE, co-operative associations, the MICH, peasant unions – and other popular forces mobilized against the law, with the support of the progressive Church (the conservative bishops sided with the government). For two weeks, the rural areas of Ecuador were in a semi-insurrectional state: *en masse* the Indian communities cut roads, stopped traffic and demonstrated in the towns. The Army tried in vain to suppress the movement by arresting some of the leaders, closing the Church radio stations that supported the Indians, and sending troops to open the roads. Only through outright civil war could the Indian uprising be crushed: the government was forced to retreat and to introduce substantial modifications to the agrarian law.[8]

While the Indian rebellion was neither 'led' nor 'promoted' by the progressive Church, liberationist Christianity – represented by Monsignor Proaño, his pastoral agents and his successor – was certainly a crucial factor in developing a new awareness and stimulating self-organization among the Quechua communities.

The main challenge to liberationist Christianity is Rome's neo-conservative offensive in Latin America. This is, of course, part of a universal process of 'restoration' in the Catholic Church, leading to an increasingly authoritarian centralization of power, to the marginalization or exclusion of dissidents, and to a doctrinal emphasis on tradition – particularly in the area of sexual morality: divorce, contraception, abortion. The recent (January 1995) removal of Monsignor Jacques Gaillot, a progressive and nonconformist French bishop from his episcopal seat – a measure unprecedented since 1945 – is only the latest sign of this growth of intolerance and conservatism.

The decisive weapon in the hands of the Vatican against doctrinal 'deviations' and 'excessively political' pastoral agents is the nomination of conservative bishops, known for their open hostility to liberation theology. Selected by the papal nuncios as 'trustworthy', these new clerics are designated by Rome to replace the retired or dead bishops who used to support socially committed pastoral activity. Several of these new bishops are members of Opus Dei, the arch-reactionary movement founded in 1928 by the Spanish priest Escriba de Balaguer (recently beatified by Rome), and well known for its widespread capitalist connections and its strong participation in the Franco regime after the war. The

Vatican has nominated seven Opus Dei priests as bishops in Peru, four in Chile, two in Ecuador, one in Colombia, Venezuela, Argentina and Brazil – and also, as we saw above, the Archbishop of San Salvador.[9] Obviously, this Roman policy creates an increasingly difficult situation for the action of liberationist Christians within the Church.

At the same time, several measures are taken against radical clerics or theologians, who are either expelled from their religious orders – such as the Cardenal brothers in Nicaragua, or Father Aristide in Haiti – or so heavily sanctioned that they prefer to leave by themselves: for example, Leonardo Boff, in 1992, having being forbidden to teach and dismissed from his position as editor of the Brazilian Catholic journal *Vozes*. In a similar logic of repression, seminaries known for their progressive spirit were, pure and simply, closed, as happened in 1989 to two important Brazilian centres: the Second Regional Seminar of the North-East (SERENE 2) and the Recife Institute of Theology (ITER).

Special treatment was reserved for the CLAR, the Confederation of Latin American Religious Orders, whose liberationist documents and pastoral orientations transformed it into a sort of alternative to the CELAM leadership (in the hands of the conservatives since 1972). In February 1989 Rome condemned 'Word and Life', a project of biblical studies in popular areas elaborated by CLAR, with the help of well-known Latin American biblicists (such as the Brazilian Carlos Mesters). A few months later, in July, Rome installed a non-elected general secretary to lead the CLAR, in open violation of its statutes.

At the same time, Rome gives full support and encouragement to conservative currents inside the Latin American Church: not only Opus Dei, which is mainly a secretive elite network, but also mass movements such as Focolari, and above all the so-called 'Charismatic Renewal' – a powerful (four million members in Brazil) movement of socially non-committed emotional religiosity that preaches total obedience to Rome's authority, and whose rituals have a strong similarity to those of the evangelical Churches: chanting, dancing, emotional expression, faith healing, public prayer at mass meetings.

The aim of this general strategy, as we saw, is the 'normalization' of the Latin American Church and the dismantling, marginalization or neutralization of its radical and liberationist wing. The Conference of Latin American Bishops held in Santo Domingo

(1992) was intended by the Vatican to become a sort of historical watershed in the theological and pastoral orientation of the continental Church, away from the tradition of Medellín and Puebla towards a realignment with Rome. Let us try to assess the religious meaning and socio-political implications of this historical event.

Inevitably, there was intersection between the preparations for the Santo Domingo Conference and the debate in Latin America about the quincentenary of the discovery of the Americas. Inside the Church two distinct conceptions became evident: one represented by the Vatican and the CELAM leadership (with some differences between them) and the other by liberation theologists.

In 1984 John Paul II, during a visit to Santo Domingo, called upon Christians to celebrate Columbus's arrival in America as 'the greatest and most marvellous human action ever' (a quote from Leo XIII in 1892), that could serve as an inspiring example for a 'new evangelization'. While denouncing the 'black legend' – which insists on the violence and exploitation in the history of the Spanish *conquista* – the Pope acknowledged that there were 'contradictions, lights and shadows' in this history, and that there had existed a regrettable interdependence between the cross and the sword during the first evangelization of the continent. Ultimately, however, the important fact was that 'the expansion of Iberian Christianity brought to the new populations the gift that was at the origin of Europe – the Christian faith, with its power of humanity, salvation, dignity and fraternity, justice and love for the New World.'[10]

The (conservative) leadership of the CELAM (Latin American Bishops Council) not only shared this positive assessment of the discovery/evangelization but even went beyond it, by suppressing any doubts, subtle qualifications or references to 'shadows'. In its message for the quicentenary of July 1984, signed by its president, Antonio Quarracino, its secretary, Dario Castrillon, and three other prelates, it does not hesitate to glorify the Hispanic conquest:

> The enterprise of the discovery, conquest and colonization of America . . . was the work of a world in which the word of Christianity still had a real content. . . . Evangelization started immediately, from the moment when Columbus took posession of the new lands in the name of the kings of Spain. The presence and action of the Church in these lands, throughout these five hundred years, is an admirable example of abnegation and perseverance, that does not need any apologetic argument to be conveniently weighed.[11]

Poles apart from this sort of self-satisfied conformism, liberationist Christians proposed a very different view of the quincentenary. In July 1986, in Quito, Ecuador, the Second Ecumenical Consultation of the Latin American Indian Pastoral took place, which issued an 'Indian Manifesto' signed by representatives of thirty indigenous nations from thirteen countries in the continent, with the support of Catholic (CIMI – Indian Missionary Council) and Protestant (CLAI – Latin American Council of Churches) bodies. This document voices 'a total rejection of these triumphalist celebrations' and forcefully challenges the official history:

> there has been no discovery as some want us to believe but rather an invasion, with the following consequences: (a) extermination by fire and blood of more than seventy-five million of our brothers; (b) violent usurpation of our territorial possessions: (c) disintegration of our socio-political and cultural institutions. . . .

Monsignor Leonidas Proaño, the Ecuadorian 'Bishop of the Indians', celebrated this document as the authentic voice of the American indigenous peoples, for whom the quincentenary 'should not be the object of pompous and triumphalist festivities, as is intended by the governments and Churches of Spain, Europe and Latin America.[12]

Another body that took a sharply critical stance was the CEHILA, Commission for the Study of the Church in Latin America, whose main leaders (like Enrique Dussel) are known for their sympathy for liberation theology. In a statement issued on 12 October 1989, CEHILA completely dissociated itself from the Christianity of the *conquistadores*:

> The invaders, in order to legitimate their arrogant pretension to superiority in the world, used the Christian God, transforming him into a symbol of power and oppression. . . . This was, we think, the idolatry of the West.

Instead of celebrating the discovery, CEHILA proposed instead to commemorate the rebellions against colonization and slavery, from Tupac Amaru to Zumbi, as well as the memory of those Christians who 'heard the cries of pain and protest, from Bartolomé de Las Casas to Oscar Romero'.[13]

Gustavo Gutiérrez contributed to the debate by writing *God or the Gold in the Indies (XVIth century)* (published in Lima in 1989) – a remarkable theological and historical study of the fight of Las

Casas in defence of the Indians against the conquerors' idolatry of gold. In an article written in the same year, dealing directly with the issue of the quincentenary, he proposed that the Santo Domingo Conference be used as a historic opportunity for Christians to 'humbly ask forgiveness of God and of the victims of history for our complicity – explicit or tacit, in the past and in the present, as persons and as a Church'.[14]

The historical issue – with its obvious theological and political implications for the present – and in particular the proposition of 'asking forgiveness' was one of the most controversial questions during the Santo Domingo Conference. Loaded with heavy symbolic and emotional content, it became the subject of an open battle between the progressive Church, headed by the Brazilian bishops, and the conservative one, strongly supported by the Roman Curia – both sides claiming to have the Pope on their side. The main episodes in this 'war of gods' were:

1. The Brazilian CNBB approved (among its directives for the conference, adopted in 1992), a powerful and explicit resolution, admitting that the Church committed 'many mistakes' during the first evangelization in Latin America, and asking the indigenous and black population of the continent for forgiveness for its 'open or hidden complicity or omission with its conquerors and oppressors'. It also acknowledged that the mistakes from the past 'still persist under various circumstances to the present day'.[15] Several other episcopal conferences (Guatemala, Bolivia) adopted similar resolutions.

2. During the conference (on 17 October 1992), thirty-three Brazilian bishops proposed a penitential liturgy, solemnly asking the Indians and Afro-Americans for forgiveness. The chair of the conference (appointed by Rome) refused the proposition and did not even submit it to the vote of the assembly.

3. The historical commission which functioned during the conference, headed by Cardinal Goicoechea from Madrid, with the help of a Spanish Vatican expert, Father Saranayana (a member of Opus Dei), drafted a long document, strongly celebrating the 'first evangelization' and not mentioning the name of Las Casas. It included a brief quote from a speech of the Pope in Africa asking forgiveness for the sin of slavery, but made no reference to the oppression of the American Indians.

4. Considered unsatisfactory by the vast majority of the conference, the historical chapter was refused! This is the only

example of global rejection of a chapter by the Latin American bishops.

5. The historical commission produced a much shorter (one and half page) section which mentioned the suffering and oppression of the indigenous population, but did not include any criticism of the Church's behaviour during the conquest.

6. Ironically enough, while the Roman representatives at the conference and their Latin American friends battled against the symbolic pardon, the Pope himself, back in Rome after his inaugural speech in Santo Domingo, gave an audience on 21 October, at which he asked the Indians and African slaves for forgiveness for the injustices committed against them.

7. A brief reference to the Pope's audience was included in the final document of the Santo Domingo Conference – not in the historical section, but in the chapter dealing with the plurality of cultures: 'together with the Pope we ask forgiveness of our indigenous and Afro-American brothers'.[16]

This whole episode is representative of the tensions and contradictions during the conference, between conservatives and progressives, the chair – headed by the the Vatican's representative, Cardinal Angelo Sodano, former nuncio in Chile, where he used to have cordial relations with General Pinochet – and the assembly, the Roman Curia and the Latin American bishops – with the Pope, predictably, as supreme arbiter.

These tensions were also present during the four years of preparation for the conference. The first documents confidentially circulated among the bishops by the CELAM leadership were strongly criticized by the local episcopal conferences for their conservative character. These papers presented the Latin American Church as the inheritor of Leo XIII's *Rerum Novarum* (1891), 'a Christian countermessage to the war cry of Marxism'. In 1991, the first official preparatory text was published, under the title *Consultation Document*: its historical section accused Las Casas of being responsible for the 'black legend' of the Spanish colonization, and in its analysis of the contemporary Latin American situation it rejected both 'the neo-liberal mentality' and 'the socialist conception'. This text was also considered inadequate (although better than the former) by the episcopal conferences: they produced written contributions, which were assembled in a collection called *Secunda Relatio*, and directly inspired the last preparatory paper

– the *Working Document*, a relatively faithful reflection of the common views of most Latin American bishops. However, during the Conference of Santo Domingo, the Draft Commission nominated by the chair practically ignored the *Working Document* and produced a new text, following a quite different method and orientation! The final document resulted from this version, substantially amended and corrected by the delegates.

How can one assess the essential meaning of the document? Did it really, as the most conservative wing of the Church, both in Rome and in Latin America wished, close the parenthesis opened in 1968 by Medellín, putting an end to the specific identity of the Latin American Church? As usual, the document was a compromise which did not quite satisfy either the progressive or the regressive tendencies. Among liberation theologians there are widely different viewpoints, but there is a sort of consensus that, at least, there had been no *radical* break with the spirit of Medellín and Puebla.

Clodovis Boff is a brilliant representative of the more critical assessment. In his opinion, there are many negative features in the final document of the conference: the traditional method of the pastoral texts – 'seeing, judging, acting' – is abandoned for a doctrinal approach, each section starting with references to papal statements; the language of liberation has practically disappeared, being replaced by a much vaguer concept of 'human advancement'; social injustice is criticized, but no reference is made to capitalism: the crime is denounced, but not the criminals; the poor appear as objects of attention rather than as subjects of their history; no mention is made of the Christian martyrs, such as Monsignor Romero or the seven Jesuit lecturers of the Salvadorean UCA; no public gesture of asking forgiveness is made, and no support is given to Rigoberta Menchù on the occasion of her receiving the Nobel Prize.

However, according to Clodovis Boff, not everything at the conference was negative: the section on 'human advancement' – where the Brazilian bishops and theologians were able to exert some influence – insisted on the need for 'structural transformation', and reaffirmed as 'strong and irrevocable' the preferential option for the poor; the *substance* of Medellín (the commitment of the Church to social change) did not disappear, even if it took a different form; important new topics such as ecology, foreign debt, street children and the drugs traffic were included.

In conclusion, Boff thinks that Santo Domingo was 'Latin American music played on a Roman guitar': there was no break with the past (Medellín/Puebla) but a sort of re-definition. Its decisions can be helpful to the 'People of God' but there is need for an active, selective, corrective and creative reading of the document.[17]

A much more positive assessment is proposed by Gustavo Gutiérrez, who believes that the most important aspect of the Santo Domingo Conference is its strong restatement of the preferential option for the poor, in continuity with Medellín and Puebla – in spite of considerable resistance both inside and outside the Church. It is true that it was not easy to come to a consensus on the issue of asking the Indian and Afro-American peoples for forgiveness for the participation of Christians in the oppression and injustice that they suffered during the sixteenth century and later, but thanks to the Pope this was finally accepted. The final document makes reference to several 'signs of the times', which are discussed from the viewpoint of the preferential option for the poor: the issue of human rights (also violated by poverty and injustice), a call for an 'ecological ethic' against utilitarian and individualist morals, the condemnation of the 'mercantilist view' of the land and of the 'sinful structures' of modern society, and the call for an 'economy of solidarity' against the neo-liberal model which 'increases the gap between poor and rich' in Latin America. Poverty is seen by Santo Domingo as 'the most devastating and humiliating plague lived by Latin America and the Caribbean', and all Christians are invited to experience a deep personal conversion leading them to discover 'in the suffering face of the poor, the face of the Lord'.

Gustavo Gutiérrez also perceives some shortcomings: he regrets that no explicit mention is made of the Latin American martyrs, and that the reflections on women prepared by a commission during the conference were not included in the final document. Comparing Santo Domingo with the previous conferences, he concludes:

> Situated in the same doctrinal and pastoral context as Medellín and Puebla, but having neither the prophetic flight of the first nor the theological density of the second, Santo Domingo collects various points of the agenda that Latin American Christians had begun to establish during the last years. The new challenges are clearly signalled. The fruitfulness of the answers will depend . . . on the reception that we will be able to give to the Santo Domingo texts.[18]

Halfway between these two opposite poles (even if they share some important judgements), many liberation theologians strike an ambivalent note. For instance, Pablo Richard, while voicing a generally positive feeling – because Santo Domingo strengthened the consciousness and identity of being a Church of the South – sees the new orientation as contradictory: in so far as the new evangelization is reflected in christological and ecclesiological theory, it is oppressive of the Latin American Church's identity and based on a sort of 'Roman fundamentalism' that has a language similar to that of many Latin American Protestant sects; in so far as it is reflected in the practice of human advancement, culture and pastoral options, it is the expression of the most authentic and profound consciousness of the Latin American Church. Most of Pablo Richard's paper about Santo Domingo is in fact a selection of the best passages from the document, to be used as a guideline for progressive pastoral agents.[19]

In fact, and this is a viewpoint common to all three theologians, the final meaning of Santo Domingo will depend on the sort of reception and interpretation it will be given over the coming years by the various Latin American Churches. Some key events which took place after Santo Domingo, such as the election, in 1995, of a conservative (Dom Lucas Moreira Neves) as the head of the powerful Brazilian Conference of Bishops – a change bound to have consequences for the whole Latin American Church – seem to indicate that the Vatican will be in a strong position to impose its own reading of the conference's documents.

In conclusion, it is difficult, if not impossible, to predict what will be the future of liberationist Christianity in Latin America. It depends on several unknown variables, such as the identity of the next Pope, or the kind of social and revolutionary movements that will impact on the continent in the next years. One cannot exclude, of course, a weakening, decline or even disappearence of the movement – although, as we saw, this is far from being the case at the moment. In any case, it has already left its stamp on the history of Latin America during the second half of the twentieth century, as a decisive protagonist of the most important social upsurges of the last thirty-five years, particularly in Brazil and in Central America. Liberationist Christianity has shaped the religious and political culture of several generations of Christian activists in the continent, most of whom are not likely to give up their deeply rooted ethical and social convictions. Moreover, it has contributed to the rise of a multiplicity of non-confessional social and political movements, from local associations in shantytowns to workers' parties or liberation fronts, which are autonomous from the Church and now have their own dynamics. A seed has been sown by liberationist Christianity in the hotbed of Latin American political and religious culture, which will continue to grow and flourish in the coming decades, and still holds many surprises in store.

Notes

Translations are mine unless otherwise specified.

Introduction

1 Max Weber, 'Science as a Vocation', 1919, in H.H. Gerth and C.W. Mills, eds, *From Max Weber*, London: Routledge, 1967, p. 152.
2 For instance, see Hugo Assmann, Franz Hinkelammert, Jorge Pixley, Pablo Richard and Jon Sobrino, *La lucha de los dioses. Los ídolos de la opresión y la búsqueda del Dios Libertador*, San José (Costa Rica), DEI (Departamento Ecumenico de Investigaciones), 1980. The name of Max Weber is not mentioned in this brilliant collection of essays.

1. Religion and Politics: Revisiting Marx and Weber

1 Quoted in Helmut Gollwitzer, 'Marxistische Religionskritik und christlicher Glaube', *Marxismusstudien*, fourth edition, Tübingen: J.C.B. Mohr, 1962, pp. 15–16. Other references to this expression can be found in this article.
2 Karl Marx, 'Towards the Critique of Hegel's *Philosophy of Right*' (1844), in Louis S. Feuer, ed., *Marx and Engels, Basic Writings on Politics and Philosophy*, London: Fontana, 1969, p. 304.
3 Karl Marx and Friedrich Engels, *The German Ideology*, in ibid., p. 50.
4 Karl Marx, *Das Kapital*, Berlin: Dietz Verlag, 1968, vol. 1, p. 96.
5 Marx, *Das Kapital*, pp. 749–50; *Foundations of the Critique of Political Economy (Rough Draft)*, Harmondsworth: Penguin, 1973, p. 232; and *Grundrisse der Kritik der Politischen Ökonomie*, Berlin: Dietz Verlag, p. 143.
6 Karl Marx, *Werke*, Berlin: Dietz Verlag, 1960, vol. 9, p. 226, and vol. 26, p. 488. Some liberation theologians (Enrique Dussel, Hugo Assmann) make extensive use of these references in their definition of capitalism as idolatry.
7 Friedrich Engels, 'Ludwig Feuerbach and the End of Classical German Philosophy', in Feuer, ed., *Marx and Engels, Basic Writings*, p. 281.
8 Friedrich Engels, 'The Peasant War in Germany', in ibid., pp. 422–75.

9 Friedrich Engels, *Anti-Dühring*, London: Lawrence & Wishart, 1969, pp. 121–2, 407.

10 Friedrich Engels, 'Contribution to a History of Primitive Christianity', in Marx and Engels, *On Religion*, London: Lawrence & Wishart, 1960, ch. 25.

11 Friedrich Engels, 'The Peasant War in Germany', 1850, in Feur, ed., *Marx and Engels, Basic Writings*, p. 464.

12 Friedrich Engels, 'On Materialism', in ibid., p. 99.

13 Karl Kautsky, *Vorläufer des neueren Sozialismus. Erster Band. Kommunistische Bewegungen im Mittelalter*, Stuttgart: Dietz Verlag, 1913, pp. 170, 198, 200–202.

14 Karl Kautsky, *Der Kommunismus in der deutschen Reformation*, Stuttgart: Dietz Verlag, 1921, pp. 3, 5.

15 Karl Kautsky, *Thomas More und seine Utopie*, Stuttgart: Dietz Verlag, 1890, pp. 101, 244–9, 325–30.

16 V.I. Lenin, 'Socialism and Religion' (1905), in *Collected Works*, Moscow: Progress, 1972, vol. 10, p. 86.

17 Rosa Luxemburg, 'Kirche und Sozialismus' (1905), in *Internationalismus und Klassenkampf*, Neuwied: Luchterhand, 1971, pp. 45–7, 67–75.

18 On this see David McClellan's interesting and useful book *Marxism and Religion*, New York: Harper & Row, ch. 3.

19 See Agnès Rochefort-Turquin's excellent research *Socialistes parce que chrétiens*, Paris: Cerf, 1986.

20 Antonio Gramsci, 'Carlo Péguy ed Ernesto Psichari' (1916), in *Scritti Giovanili 1914–1918*, Turin: Einaudi, 1958, pp. 33–4; 'I movimenti e Coppoleto' (1916), in *Sotto la Mole*, Turin: Einaudi, 1972, pp. 118–19. Gramsci also seemed interested, in the early 1920s, by the peasant movement led by a leftist Catholic, G. Miglioli. See on this the remarkable book by Rafael Diaz-Salazar, *El proyecto de Gramsci*, Barcelona: Anthropos, pp. 96–7.

21 Antonio Gramsci, *Selections from the Prison Notebooks*, ed. Quintin Hoare and G. Nowell Smith, London: New Left Books, 1971, pp. 328, 397, 405; *Il Materialismo Storico*, Rome: Editori Riuniti, 1979, p. 17.

22 Gramsci, *Il Materialismo Storico*, pp. 17–18 (direct reference to Weber), 50, 110. See also M. Montanari, 'Razionalità e tragicità del moderno in Gramsci', *Critica Marxista*, 2–3, 1987, p. 58.

23 Gramsci, *Il Materialismo Storico*, p. 105. See also Kautsky, *Thomas More und seine Utopie*, p. 76.

24 Ernst Bloch, *Das Prinzip Hoffnung*, Frankfurt/Main: Suhrkamp Verlag, 1959, 3 vols; *Atheismus im Christentum. Zur Religion des Exodus und des Reichs*, Frankfurt/Main: Suhrkamp Verlag, 1968.

25 Max Horkheimer, 'Gedanke zur Religion' (1935), in *Kritische Theorie*, Frankfurt/Main: S. Fischer Verlag, 1972, vol. 1, p. 374.

26 See Michael Löwy 'Revolution against Progress: Walter Benjamin's Romantic Anarchism', *New Left Review*, no. 152, November–December 1985; and 'Religion, Utopia and Countermodernity: The Allegory of the Angel of History in Walter Benjamin', in Michael Löwy, *On Changing the World*, Atlantic Highlands, NJ: Humanities Press, 1993.

27 McLellan, *Marxism and Religion*, p. 128.

28 Lucien Goldmann, *Le Dieu caché*, Paris: Gallimard, 1955, p. 99.

29 José Carlos Mariátegui, 'El hombre y el mito' (1925), in *El alma matinal*, Lima: Amauta, 1971, pp. 18–22; and *Defensa del Marxismo* (1930), Lima: Amauta, 1971, p. 21.

30 For a detailed discussion of this concept and its methodological usefulness for the sociology of culture, see Michael Löwy, *Redemption and Utopia*:

Libertarian Judaism in Central Europe, Stanford, CA; Stanford University Press, 1993.

31 Max Weber, *The Protestant Ethic and the Spirit of Capitalism*, London: Unwin, 1967, pp. 73–4.

32 Max Weber, *Die protestantische Ethik II. Kritiken und Antikritiken*, Gütersloh: GTB, 1972, p. 168.

33 Max Weber, 'Zwischenbetrachtung', in *Die Wirtschaftsethik der Weltreligionen. Konfuzianismus und Taoismus*, Tübingen: J.C.B. Mohr, 1989, pp. 487–8.

34 Max Weber, *Wirtschaft und Gesellschaft*, Tübingen: J.C.B.Mohr, 1923, p. 305. In another chapter of the book Weber speaks of the 'deepest antipathy' of all hierocratic religions (including Catholicism) towards capitalism, motivated by the impossibility of any ethical control of the system:

> In contrast to all other forms of domination, the economic domination of capital cannot, because of its 'impersonal character', be ethically regulated. . . . The competitiveness, the market, the labour market, the monetary market, the commodity market, in one word 'objective' considerations, neither ethical nor anti-ethical, but simply non-ethical . . . determine behaviour at the decisive points and push between the involved human beings impersonal instances. (Ibid., pp. 708–9).

35 Max Weber, *Wirtschaftsgeschichte*, Munich: Dunker & Humbolt, 1923, p. 305. The Latin quotation may be translated as: 'The merchant may triumph, but he can never please God.'

36 Ibid., p. 306.

37 See Bernard Groethuysen, *The Bourgeois. Catholicism vs. Capitalism in Eighteenth-Century France*, New York: Holt, Rinehart & Winston, pp. 192–3, 217. Groethuysen begins his study with the seventeenth century, but there are enough other works that refer to earlier periods. According to J. Strieder, in the seventeenth century there existed widespread expressions of a passionate Catholic opposition to the early forms of the capitalist spirit [*früh kapitalistischen Geist*]. See his book *Studien zur Geschichte kapitalistischen Organisationsformen*, Munich 1925, p. 63.

38 See Jean-Pierre Gutton, *La Société et les pauvres. L'exemple de la généralité de Lyon 1534–1789*, Paris: Les Belles Lettres, 1971.

39 Émile Poulat, *Église contre bourgeoisie. Introduction au devenir du catholicisme social actuel*, Paris: Castermann, 1977. The quote from Laveleye's book *Le Socialisme contemporain* (Paris: Alcan, 1888, p. 167) may be found in Émile Poulat, *Journal d'un prêtre d'après demain*, Paris: Castermann, 1961, p. 187.

40 Bolívar Echevarría, 'El ethos barroco', *Nariz del diablo*, Quito (Ecuador), no. 20, p. 40.

41 Amintore Fanfani, *Catholicism, Protestantism and Capitalism* (1935), Notre Dame, IN: University of Notre Dame Press, 1984.

42 Ibid., pp. 142–51, 208.

43 Michael Novak, 'Introduction: The Catholic Anti-capitalist Bias', in Fanfani, p. xlviii.

44 Michael Novak, *The Spirit of Democratic Capitalism*, New York: Touchstone, 1982, pp. 25, 239, 242.

45 Thomas More, *Utopia*, New York: Washington Square Press, 1965, pp. 14–16.

46 Karl Marx, 'Manifesto of the Communist Party', in *The Revolution of 1848*, Harmondsworth: Penguin, 1973, p. 88.

47 Johannes von Baader, 'Über das dermalige Missverhältnis der Vermögenlosen oder Proletairs zu den Vermögen besitzenden Klassen der

Sozietät in betreff ihres Auskommens sowohl in materieller als intellektueller Hinsicht aus dem Standpunkte des Rechts betrachtet' (1835), in G.K. Kaltenbrunner, ed., *Sätze sur Erotische Philosophie*, Frankfurt: Insel Verlag, 1991, pp. 181-2, 186. We are not dealing here with the numerous 'Christian communists' of the early nineteenth century (Cabet, Weitling, Kriege) because they had few links to Catholicism or the Church. The best reference in this area is Henri Desroche, *Socialismes et sociologie religieuse*, Paris: Cujas, 1965.

48 On this see on Michael Löwy and Robert Sayre, *Révolte et mélancolie. Le romantisme à contre-courant de la modernité*, Paris: Payot, 1992.

49 Ernst Bloch, *Thomas Münzer als Theologue der Revolution*, Frankfurt/ Main: Suhrkamp Verlag, 1972, pp. 118-19. In a similar vein, Erich Fromm, in an essay from the 1930s, referred to Sombart and Weber to denounce the role of Calvinism in establishing the duties to work, to acquire commodities and to save as the dominant bourgeois ethical norms – instead of the inborn right to happiness acknowledged by pre-capitalist societies (such as medieval Catholic culture). See Erich Fromm, 'Die psychoanalytische Charakterologie und ihre Bedeutung für die Sozialpsychologie', *Zeitschrift für Sozialforschung*, 1932, in E. Fromm, *Gesamtausgabe*, Stuttgart: Deutsche Verlag-Anstalt, 1980, I, pp. 59–77.

50 Emmanuel Mounier, *Feu la chretienté*, Paris: Seuil, 1950, p. 52. During the 1930s, Mounier seemed both fascinated and terrified by some so-called 'leftist' tendencies in fascism, and his attitude to Vichy's 'national revolution' in 1940 was ambivalent. Soon afterwards he joined the Resistance and after the war he became increasingly attracted by Marxism.

51 H. de Vaz Lima, 'La Jeunesse brésilienne à l'heure des décisions', *Perspectives de catholicité*, no. 4, 1963, p. 288.

52 Resolutions of the JOC and ACO (Workers' Catholic Action) Congress, Recife, 15 June 1968, quoted in Marcio Moreira Alves, *L'Église et la politique au Brésil*, Paris: Cerf, 1974, p. 153.

53 Herbert José de Souza, 'Juventude cristã hoje', in *Cristianismo hoje*, Rio de Janeiro: Editôra Universitaria da UNE, 1962, pp. 110, 112.

2. Liberationist Christianity in Latin America

1 This precision has become necessary as certain sociologists, taking the pretext of the insufficiently 'integrated' and 'well co-ordinated' character of this network, deny the existence of a social movement: according to Jean Daudelin, for instance, 'this movement has been nothing but a theological utopia and a sociological fiction' ('Brazil's Progressive Church in Crisis: Institutional weakness and political vulnerability', manuscript, 1991).

2 Max Weber, 'Zwischenbetrachtung', in *Die Wirtschaftsethik der Weltreligionen. Konfuzianismus und Taoismus*, Tübingen: J.C.B. Mohr, 1989, pp. 485-6. English: 'Religious rejections of the world and their directions', in H.H. Gerth and C.W. Mills, eds, *From Max Weber*, London: Routledge, 1967, p. 329.

3 Gustavo Gutiérrez, *Théologie de la libération – perspectives*, Brussels: Lumen Vitae, 1974, p. 261.

4 Max Weber, 'The social psychology of the world religions', in Gerth and Mills, eds, *From Max Weber*, pp. 276-7.

5 Daniel Levine, ed., *Churches and Politics in Latin America*, Beverly Hills, CA: Sage, 1980, pp. 17–19, 30; and Daniel Levine, ed., *Religion and*

Political Conflict in Latin America, Chapel Hill: The University of North Carolina Press, 1986, p. 17.

6 Henri Desroche, *Sociologie de l'espérance*, Paris, Calmann-Lévy, 1973, p. 158.

7 Definition of believing [*croire*] by Danièle Hervieu-Léger, *La religion pour mémoire*, Paris: Cerf, 1993, p. 105. The idea of a common matrix of religion and politics which regulates 'the passages from one into the other according to very complex mechanisms of mutual reloading and redefining' appears in Patrick Michel's recent book *Politique et religion. La grande mutation*, Paris: Albin Michel, 1994, p. 27. Michel de Certeau had already written about the 'complex movement back and forth between religion and politics' (and specifically Christianity and socialism), through which a transfer of beliefs takes place within the same structural outline. See his book *L'Invention du quotidien. 1. Arts de faire* (1980), Paris: Gallimard-Folio, 1990, pp. 265–8 as well as pp. 261–4, where he writes about the shifts, transitions and investments of the believing energy [*énergie croyante*].

8 Lucien Goldmann, *Le Dieu caché*, Paris: Gallimard, 1955, p. 99; see also the English edition, *The Hidden God*, London: Routledge & Kegan Paul, 1964, p. 90.

9 Pedro. A. Ribeiro de Oliveira, 'Estruturas de Igreja e conflitos religiosos', in Pierre Sanchis, ed., *Catolicismo: modernidade et tradição*, São Paulo: Loyola/ ISER, 1992, p. 54. This is a most valuable collection of essays by the Research Group on Brazilian Catholicism from the ISER, the Institute for the Study of Religion, Rio de Janeiro.

10 Thomas C. Bruneau, 'Church and Politics in Brazil: The Genesis of Change', *Journal of Latin American Studies*, Cambridge University Press, no. 17, November 1985, pp. 286–9.

11 See for example Luis Alberto Gómez de Souza's remarkable work *Classes populares e Igreja nos caminhos da historia*, Petrópolis: Vozes, 1982, p. 240. For an interesting critical assessment of these two approaches, see Sanchis, 'Introdução', *Catolicismo: modernidade e tradição*, pp. 23–7.

12 Leonardo Boff, *Igreja, carisma e poder*, Petrópolis: Vozes, 1986, p. 178.

13 My translation of the term *pobretariado* used by Christian trade unionists in Latin America.

14 Danièle Hervieu-Léger, *Vers un nouveau christianisme?*, Paris: Cerf, 1986, pp. 312–17.

15 Jean Séguy, 'Une Sociologie des sociétés imaginées: monachisme et utopie', *Annales ESC*, March–April 1971, pp. 337, 354.

16 Brian H. Smith, *The Church and Politics in Chile: Challenges to Modern Catholicism*, Princeton, NJ: Princeton University Press, 1982, p. 248.

17 See his book *Opresión-Liberación, desafío à los cristianos*, Montevideo: Tierra Nueva, 1971.

18 A very good summary of this background can be found in Enrique Dussel, *Teologia de la liberación. Un panorama de su desarrollo*, Mexico: Potrerillos Editores, 1995.

19 Gustavo Gutiérrez, *Théologie de la libération*, pp. 39–40.

20 Gonzalo Arroyo, 'Consideraciones sobre el subdesarrollo en América Latina', *Cuadernos de CEREN*, no. 5, 1970, p. 61.

21 *Christians for Socialism. Documentation of the Christians for Socialism Movement in Latin America*, New York (Maryknoll): Orbis, 1975, p. 173.

22 See Daniel Levine, 'Assessing the Impacts of Liberation Theology in Latin America', *The Review of Politics*, University of Notre Dame, spring 1988, p. 252.

23 Carol Drogus, 'Reconstructing the feminine: women in São Paulo's CEBs',

Archives des sciences sociales des religions, no. 71, July–September 1990, pp. 63–74.

24 Pedro de Oliveira, 'Estruturas de Igreja e conflitos religiosos', p. 58.

25 See the interesting article by Ana Maria Doimo, 'Igreja e movimentos sociais post-70 no Brasil', in Sanchis, ed., *Catolicismo: cotidiano e movimentos*, pp. 275–308.

26 Levine, ed., *Religion and Political Conflict in Latin America*, p. 15. Weber's reference is taken from *Economy and Society*, Berkeley: University of California Press, 1978, vol. 1, p. 591. See also Levine's interesting book *Popular Voices in Latin American Catholicism*, Princeton, NJ: Princeton University Press, 1992.

27 Yvo do Amaral Lesbaupin, 'Mouvement populaire, Église catholique et politique au Brésil: l'apport des communautés ecclésiales urbaines de base aux mouvements populaires', doctoral thesis, Toulouse, 1987, p. 341 (this remarkable PhD has unfortunately not yet been published). The Weber reference is from *Economy and Society*: 'Die innere Wahlverwandtschaft mit der Struktur der Demokratie liegt schon in diesen eigenen Strukturprinzipien der Sekte auf der Hand'. M. Weber, *Wirtschaft und Gesellschaft*, Tübingen, J.C.B. Mohr, 1922, p. 815.

28 Frei Betto, 'Método y pedagogía de las comunidades ecleisales de base', *Diálogo* (Costa Rica), no. 8, 1982 (quoted from a French translation: 'Populisme et avant-gardisme ecclésiaux', COELI, Brussels, no. 2, September 1982, p. 2).

29 Boff, *Igreja, carisma e poder*, p. 94; and Gustavo Gutiérrez, *La Force historique des pauvres*, Paris: Cerf, 1986, pp. 178–84.

30 Boff, *Igreja, carisma e poder*, pp. 41, 72–5.

31 Gutiérrez, *La Force historique*, p. 261.

32 Elsa Tamez, ed., *Teólogos de la liberación hablan sobre la mujer*, Costa Rica: DEI, 1986.

33 Gustavo Gutiérrez, 'Théologie et sciences sociales', in *Théologies de la libération*, Paris: Cerf, 1985, p. 193.

34 Pablo Richard, 'L'Église entre la modernité et la libération', *Parole et société*, 1978, pp. 32–3.

35 Hugo Assmann, Franz Hinkelammert, Jorge Pixley, Pablo Richard and Jon Sobrino, *La lucha de los dioses. Los ídolos de la opresión y la búsqueda del Dios libertador*, San José de Costa Rica: DEI, 1980.

36 Jung Mo Sung, *A idolatria do capital e a morte dos pobres*, São Paulo: Edições Paulinas, 1989; and *Teologia & economia. Repensando a teologia da libertação e as utopias*, Petrópolis: Vozes, 1995.

37 Hugo Assmann and Franz Hinkelammert, *A idolatria do mercado. Ensaio sobre economia e teologia*, São Paulo: Vozes, 1989.

38 Gustavo Gutiérrez, 'Liberation Praxis and Christian Faith', in Rosino Gibellini, ed., *Frontiers of Theology in Latin America*, New York (Maryknoll): Orbis, 1983, pp. 1–2.

39 Hervieu-Léger, *Vers un nouveau christianisme?*, p. 299.

40 Gutiérrez, *La Force historique*, p. 187.

41 Ivan Vallier, 'Radical Priests and Revolution', in O. Chalmers, ed., *Change in Latin America: New Interpretations of its Politics and Society*, New York: Academy of Political Sciences, 1972, pp. 17–23.

42 Juan Carlos Scannone, 'Théologie et politique', in Dussel, Gutiérrez *et al.*, *Les Luttes de libération bousculent la théologie*, Paris: Cerf, 1975, pp. 144–8.

43 Gutiérrez, *La Force historique*, p. 187.

44 Ibid., pp. 172–3, 218.

45 Marcello Azevedo, SJ, *Comunidades eclesiais de base e inculturação da fé*, São Paulo: Loyola, ch. II.1.

46 Harvey Cox, *Religion in the Secular City. Toward a Post-Modern Theology*, New York: Simon & Schuster, 1984, pp. 103, 215.

47 Leonardo Boff, *Église en genèse. Les communautés de base*, Paris: Desclée, 1978, pp. 7-21.

48 Cox, *Religion in the Secular City*, p. 127.

49 Jean Séguy, 'Protestations socio-religieuses et contre-culture', EPHE seminar paper, 1973-74, unpublished mimeo, p. 11.

50 Hugo Assmann, *Theology for a Nomad Church*, New York (Maryknoll): Orbis, 1976, pp. 49-50; and Gutiérrez, *Théologie de la libération*, p. 92 - see also pp. 39-40, 90-91.

51 'Denuncia de três bispos do vale São Francisco', in *Pastoral da Terra*, Estudos CNBB, no. 11, São Paulo: Edições Paulinas, 1981, p. 187-8, and *O mausoléu do Faraó*, Curitiba: CPT, 1979.

52 See, for instance, the work of the Ecumenical Centre for Documentation and Research (CEDI) published in July 1989, under the title 'The State and Land: trade-unions, dams, agro-industry', in the journal *Tempo e Presença* (Rio de Janeiro).

53 Jeanne Bisilliat, 'Un mouvement populaire à S. Paulo et son équipe technique architecturale', *Cahiers de l'ORSTOM*, Paris, 1989.

54 Hugo Assmann, *A Igreja eletrônica e seu impacto na América Latina*, Petrópolis: Vozes, 1986, pp. 172-6.

55 Christian Duquoc, *Libération et progressisme*, Paris: Cerf, 1988, pp. 28-96.

56 See Roberto Romano, *Brasil: Igreja contra estado. Critica ao populismo católico*, São Paulo: Kairos, 1979, pp. 173, 230-31. Romano is one of the few authors to have noted some of Weber's remarks on the tension between Catholicism and capitalism, which he has tried to apply to the Brazilian case.

57 'A New Interamerican Policy for the Eighties'.

58 'Santa Fe II. Una estrategia para A. Latina en los noventas'.

59 'Conferencia Interamericana de los Ejercitos, Punta del Este, dec. 1987, capítulo Estrategia del Movimento Comunista Internacional en Latino-américa, a través de distintos modos de acción'.

60 Cardinal Ratzinger, 'Les Conséquences fondamentales d'une option marxiste', in *Théologies de la libération*, pp. 122-30.

61 For a history and explanation of the concept, see Michael Löwy, *Redemption and Utopia: Libertarian Judaism in Central Europe*, Stanford, CA: Stanford University Press, 1993. In a recent (very insightful) work, a Brazilian theologian has used this concept (as I tried to define it) to examine the 'elective affinity' between Marxism and liberation theology: Enio Ronald Mueller, *Teologia da Libertaçâo e Marxismo: uma relaçâo em busca de explicaçâo (affection quaerens intellectum)*, Escola Superior de Teologia: São Leopoldo, 1994.

62 *Instruction sur quelques aspects de la 'théologie de la libération'*, 1984.

63 See Guy Petitdemange's excellent study, 'Théologie(s) de la libération et marxisme(s)', in 'Pourquoi la théologie de la libération', supplement to no. 307 of *Cahiers de l'actualité religieuse et sociale*, 1985. For a historical overview of the process, see also Enrique Dussel's interesting essay 'Encuentro de cristianos y marxistas en América Latina', *Cristianismo y sociedad* (Santo Domingo), no. 74, 1982.

64 Criticizing this purely 'instrumental' conception, the German lay theologian Bruno Kern tries to show that in fact the relationship with Marxism has a much broader meaning for liberation theology: *Theologie im Horizont des Marxismus. Zur Geschichte der Marxismusrezeption in der lateinamerikanis-*

chen Theologie der Befreiung, Mainz: Mathias-Grünewald Verlag, 1992, pp.14–26.

65 *Théologie de la libération*, p. 244. It is true that since 1984, following the Vatican criticisms, Gutiérrez seems to have retreated to a less exposed position, reducing the relation with Marxism to an encounter between theology and the social sciences. See Gustavo Gutiérrez, 'Théologie et sciences sociales', 1985, in *Théologies de la libération*, pp. 189–93.

66 In his outstanding book on revolutionary Christianity in Latin America, Samuel Silva Gotay mentions the following Marxist authors as significant references for liberation theology: Goldmann, Garaudy, Schaff, Kolakowski, Lukács, Gramsci, Lombardo-Radice, Luporini, Sanchez Vazquez, Mandel, Fanon and the journal *Monthly Review*. Samuel Silva Gotay, *O pensamento cristão revolucionario na América Latina e no Caribe, 1969–73*, São Paulo: Edições Paulinas, 1985, p. 232.

67 On the use of the dependency theory by liberation theologians see Luigi Bordini, *O marxismo e a teologia da libertação*, Rio de Janeiro: Editora Dois Pontos, 1987, ch. 6; and Samuel Silva Gotay, *O pensamento cristão revolucionario*, pp. 192–7.

68 *Theologie de la libération*, pp. 276–7.

69 Liberationist Christians such as the Chilean Jesuit Gonzalo Arroyo rejected the dominant conception of development as a transition from 'traditional' to 'modern' society, modernity being 'implicitly identified with the modern type of industrial capitalism'. Gonzalo Arroyo, 'Consideraciones sobre el sub-desarrollo en América Latina', Santiago: Cuadernos del CEREN, no. 5, 1970, p. 61.

70 *Documentos do Partido Comunista Brasileiro*, Lisbon: Editora Avante, 1976, p. 71.

71 *Los Obispos Latinoamericanos entre Medellín y Puebla*, San Salvador: UCA (Universidad Centroamericana), 1978, p. 71.

72 *J'ai entendu les cris de mon peuple (Exode 3.7). Documents d'évêques et supérieurs religieux du nord-est brésilien*, Brussels: Entraide et Fraternité, 1973, pp. 42–3.

73 For example, *Théologie de la libération*, pp. 102, 320. The quote from José Carlos Mariátegui is taken from the collection of essays *Ideologia e política*, Lima: Editorial Amauta, 1971, p. 249.

74 Leonardo and Clodovis Boff, 'Le Cri de la pauvreté', 1985, in *Théologies de la libération*, p. 139.

75 Otavio Guilherme Velho, *Sociedade e agricultura*, Rio de Janeiro: Zahar Editora, 1982, pp. 125–36.

76 *Théologie de la libération*, p. 266.

77 Quoted in ibid., pp. 117–18. In a footnote, Gutiérrez mentions several other Latin American episcopal documents of similar persuasion.

78 Luis Carrión, 'Les chrétiens dans la révolution sandiniste', *Inprecor*, no. 246, July 1987, p. 16.

3. Politics and Religion in Latin America: Three Examples

1 Regional Centro-Oeste, 'Algumas diretrizes de um ideal histórico cristão para o povo brasileiro', in Luis Gonzaga de Souza Lima, *Evolução política dos católicos e da Igreja*, Petrópolis: Vozes, 1979, pp. 87–92.

2 Scott Mainwaring, *The Catholic Church and Politics in Brazil 1916–1985*, Stanford, CA: Stanford University Press, 1986, p. 72. However, in another

passage of his book, Mainwaring seems to acknowledge this fact: 'The Christian left began to develop one of the first specifically latin-american theologies' (p. 72). For a more systematic discussion of this 'French/Brazilian connection' see Michael Löwy with Jesús García Ruiz, *Les sources françaises du christianisme de la libération au Brésil* (forthcoming).

3 Quoted in F. Prandini, V. Petrucci and Frei Romeu Dale OP, *As relações Igreja–estado no Brasil, vol. 1 (1964–67)*, São Paulo: Loyola, 1986, pp. 36–7.

4 Ibid., vol. 3, p. 18.

5 Mainwaring, *The Catholic Church and Politics in Brazil 1916–1985*, p. 104.

6 See Frei Betto, *Batismo de sangue. Os dominicanos e a morte de Carlos Marighella*, Rio de Janeiro: Bertrand, 1987, p. 237.

7 *As relações Igreja-estado no Brasil*, vol. 3, pp. 33–4.

8 It is quite difficult to give a precise assessment of the number of CEBs in Brazil. Estimations differ wildly: Scott Mainwaring speaks of eighty thousand communities and two million members, an evaluation shared by most authors.

9 Max Weber, 'Religious rejections of the world and their directions', in *From Max Weber*, ed. H. H. Gerth and C. W. Mills, London: Routledge, 1967, p. 330. See 'Zwischenbetrachtung', p. 486.

10 Frei Betto, *Batismo de sangue. Os dominicanos e a morte de Carlos Marighella*. One of the most interesting scenes is the one in which Betto transcribes a sort of strange 'theological confrontation' with a police agent:

How can a Christian collaborate with a communist? – For me, men are divided not into believers and atheists, but between oppressors and oppressed, between those who want to keep this unjust society and those who want to struggle for justice – Have you forgotten that Marx considered religion to be the opium of the people? – It is the bourgeoisie which has turned religion into an opium of the people by preaching a God lord of the heavens only, while taking possession of the earth for itself.

11 Charles Antoine, 'Le Démantèlement d'une Église', *Actualités religieuses du monde*, 15 November 1988.

12 Ernesto Bernardes, 'O homem do Vaticano', *Veja*, 24 May 1995, pp. 102–3.

13 From a statement issued by three American priests (Mahon, Greely and McGlinn) from San Miguelito, Panama, in January 1964. See 'A missão da Igreja na América Latina', *Revista civilização brasileira*, Rio de Janeiro, no. 3, July 1965, p. 315.

14 Comandante Padre Gaspara García Laviana, *Folletos populares Gaspar García Laviana*, no. 8, Instituto Histórico Centro-Americano, Managua, n.d.

15 Quoted in Philip Berryman, *The Religious Roots of Rebellion: Christians in Central American Revolutions*, New York (Maryknoll): Orbis, 1984, p. 77.

16 Quoted in Michael A. Gismondi, 'Transformations of the Holy: Religious Resistance and Hegemonic Struggles in the Nicaraguan Revolution', *Latin American Perspectives*, vol. 13, no. 3, summer 1986, p. 28.

17 Quoted in Berryman, p. 396.

18 Centro Ecuménico Antonio Valdivieso, 'Iglesia y revolución en Nicaragua', in G. Girardi, B. Forcano and J.M. Vigil, eds, *Nicaragua trinchera teológica*, Managua: CEAV, 1987.

19 See Carlos Rafael Cabarrus's remarkable book *Génesis de una revolución. Origen y desarrollo de la organización campesina en El Salvador*, Mexico City: Ediciones de la Casa Chata, 1982: Phillip Berryman, *The Religious Roots of Rebellion*.

20 See Universidad Centro-Americana (UCA), *Rutilio Grande, mártir de la*

evangelización rural, San Salvador, 1978: *El Salvador, un pueblo perseguido*. *Testimonio de cristianos*, Lima: CEP, 1981, p. 55.

21 Ana Carrigan, *Salvador Witness: The Life and Calling of Jean Donovan*, New York: Ballantine Books, 1984, p. 109.

22 Quoted in Placido Erdozain and Maurice Barth, *Salvador. Oscar Romero et son peuple*, Paris: Karthala, 1982, pp. 146–7. See also *La voz de los sin voz. La palabra viva de Monseñor Romero*, El Salvador: UCA, 1987; James R. Brockman, *The Word Remains: A Life of Oscar Romero*, New York (Maryknoll): Orbis, 1982.

23 Quoted in Ana Carrigan, p. 152.

24 See *In Memoriam: The Jesuit Martyrs of El Salvador*, New York (Maryknoll), Orbis, 1990, with a preface by Jon Sobrino SJ.

25 José Míguez Bonino, 'Historical Praxis and Christian Identity', in R.Gibellini, ed., *Frontiers of Theology in Latin America*, New York (Maryknoll): Orbis, 1983, pp. 261–64.

26 See *De dentro do furacão. Richard Shaull e os primordios da teologia da libertação*, São Paulo: CEDI (Centro Ecuménico de Documentação e Informação) – CLAI (Conselho Latino-Americano de Igrejas), 1985. This volume contains both recollections about Shaull and extracts from his writings.

27 Rubem Alves, *A Theology of Human Hope*, Washington, DC: Corpus Books, 1969; *Cristianismo: opio o liberación?*, Salamanca: Sigueme, 1973, pp. 177–8, 240–47. Alves first met with Gustavo Gutiérrez in Geneva in 1969, at an ecumenical conference of SODEPAX and both agreed on the need to replace the 'theology of development' with a new one based upon the concept of liberation.

28 See Julio de Santa Ana's remarkable synthesis 'Du libéralisme à la praxis de libération. Genèse de la contribution protestante à la théologie latino-américaine de la libération', *Archives de sciences sociales de la religion*, no. 71, July–September 1990.

29 T.S. Montgomery, 'Latin American Evangelicals: Oaxtepec and Beyond', in Daniel Levine ed., *Churches and Politics in Latin America*, Beverly Hills, CA: Sage, 1980, pp. 87–107.

30 Jorge V. Pixley, *Exodo*, São Paulo: Ediçôes Paulinas, 1987, p. 6; (with Clodovis Boff), *A opção pelos pobres*, São Paulo: Vozes, 1986.

31 See David Stoll, *Is Latin America Turning Protestant? The Politics of Evangelical Growth*, Berkeley: University of California Press, 1990, pp. xiv, 6, 8, 9, 101, 125. This valuable research – a first-rate piece of investigative journalism – is one of the main sources for this section.

32 Stoll, pp. 156–7. Stoll's 'five concentric circles' refer to the missionary movement, but I think they are also useful in understanding the political spectrum of the whole evangelical movement.

33 See Stephen Glazier, ed., *Perspectives on Pentecostalism: Case Studies from the Caribbean and Latin America*, Washington, DC: University Press of America; Christian Lalive d'Épinay, 'Political Regimes and Millenarianism in a Dependent Society: Reflections on Pentecostalism in Chile', *Concilium*, no. 161, New York, 1983, pp. 42–54; and Stoll, pp. 111–12.

34 Tom Barry, Deb Preusch and Beth Sims, *The New Right Humanitarians*, Albuquerque: The Resource Center, pp. 14–30. According to Deborah Huntington and Enrique Dominguez, these evangelical groups tried to dissuade Central Americans from joining movements for social change, by holding out the hope of a spiritual alternative to political action. They also assured US supporters that the Reagan administration's version of events was correct, and attacked critics as communist sympathizers ('The Salvation

Brokers: Conservative Evangelicals in Central America', *NACLA Report on the Americas* 18 (1), 1984). David Stoll comments: 'They were, in effect, cheerleaders for US military intervention. To support the Nicaraguan *contras*, they worked closely with organizations studded with former military and intelligence officers. In joining the *contra* war, they seemed bent on confirming fears that North American missions were CIA fronts' (p. 139).

35 Stoll, pp. 326–7. Stoll's comment is very illuminating:

> To those who distrust and fear evangelical growth, Oliver North and his friends have confirmed the view that it is the result of strategic US planning. That evangelism is a spiritual con game, of attracting Latin Americans with dollars, working closely with the local power structure, and following orders from Washington. This is the conspiracy explanation for evangelical growth in Latin America. . . . It is not the picture I wanted to draw when I started this book; it is the folk mythology that I wanted to refute, not affirm. Yet Oliver North and his evangelists have done this great disservice to their brethren: they have shown it is true.

36 Stoll, p. 293.

37 An evangelical living in El Salvador wrote the following comment to David Stoll: 'most Salvadorean evangelicals are poor campesinos and city dwellers, and most of them would probably describe themselves as apolitical. . . . The main political reason that the poor turn to evangelicalism is not anti-communism, but safety.' Evangelism also has an upper-class appeal in these countries among the economic elite and military families, who are attracted by a spirituality that does not criticize the social structure from which they benefit but absolves them of responsibility for it. See Stoll, pp. 167–70.

38 Stoll, pp. 2–3.

39 Quoted in Richard Gott, 'The Latin Conversion', *The Guardian Weekly*, 10 June 1995, p. 27.

40 See Michael Löwy, 'Weber against Marx?', in *On Changing the World: Essays in Political Philosophy from Karl Marx to Walter Benjamin*, Atlantic Highlands, NJ: Humanities Press, 1993.

41 For a critique of this '*faux*-Weberian optimism' from a neo-liberal viewpoint, see Timothy Goodman, 'Latin America's Reformation', *The American Enterprise*, July–August 1991.

42 See Jean-Pierre Bastian, 'The Metamorphosis of Latin American Protestant Groups: A Socio-Historical Perspective', *LARR*, vol. 28 no. 2, 1993, pp. 35, 43; and Luis E. Samandu, 'El Pentecostalismo en Nicaragua y sus raices religiosas populares', *Pasos* (San José, Costa Rica), no. 17, May–June 1988, p. 8.

43 Stoll, p. 112.

44 A detailed presentation of these events can be found in Phillip Berryman, *The Religious Roots of Rebellion: Christians in Central American Revolutions*, New York (Maryknoll): Orbis, 1984, ch. 6, 'The Color of Blood Is Never Forgotten', as well as in Rigoberta Menchù's moving testimony, *I, Rigoberta Menchù: An Indian Woman in Guatemala*, London: Verso, 1984.

45 Edward L. Cleary, 'Evangelicals and Competition in Guatemala', in Edward Cleary and Hannah Stewart-Gambino, eds, *Conflict and Competition: The Latin American Church in a Changing Environment*, Boulder, CO: Lynne Rienner Publishers, 1992, p. 188.

46 See the remarkable essays by Jesús García Ruiz, 'L'État, le religieux et le contrôle de la population indigène au Guatemala', *Revue française de science politique*, vol. 38, no. 5, October 1988; and 'Un essai de contrôle des consciences dans un contexte de guerre civile: militaires et population indienne au Guatemala', in François Chazel, ed., *Action collective et mouvements sociaux*, Paris: Presses Universitaires de France, 1993.

47 Clifford Kraus, *Inside Central America: Its People, Politics and History*, New York: Summit Books, 1991, p. 41.

48 Preaching of the Word Church, Guatemala City, April 1983. Quoted in Jesús García Ruiz, 'Le religieux comme lieu de pénétration politique et idéologique au Guatemala', *Revue française d'etudes américaines*, no. 24–25, May 1985, pp. 268–9.

49 Comisión de derechos humanos de Guatemala, *Ejecuciones masivas extrajudiciales, 1981–1985*, Mexico, 1988, mimeo. See also Jesús García Ruiz, 'Un essai de contrôle des consciences ... ', pp. 138–9; and Stoll, p. 191–2.

50 Quoted in Stoll, p. 204.

51 See ibid., pp. 131–2, 170–78.

52 On the Pentecostals in the Brazilian Peasant Leagues, see Francisco Cartaxo Rolim, *Pentecostais no Brasil. Uma interpretação sócio-religiosa*, Petrópolis: Vozes, 1985; Regina Reyes Novaes, *Os escolhidos de Deus. Pentecostais, trabalhadores e cidadania*, Rio de Janeiro: Marco Zero/ISER, 1985.

53 Paul Freston, 'A transformação política da comunidade evangélica ou (quase) tudo o que evangélicos e partidos progressistas precisam saber sobre o movimento evangélico progressista', *Vespera*, 21 November 1993.

54 Paul Freston, 'Os trabalhadores e os evangélicos', *Teoria e debate* no. 25, August 1994, pp. 23–6. See also *Boletim do MEP* no. 1, December 1993. Progressive evangelical theology is developed in books by Robinson Cavalcanti, *A utopia possivel: em busca de um cristianismo integral*, São Paulo: Editora Ultimato, 1993; Paul Freston, *Fé bíblica e crise brasileira*, São Paulo: ABU, 1993.

55 Cartaxo Rolim, p. 259; Stoll, p. 331. In a recent anthropological study on Brazil, John Burdick offers an interesting analysis of the attraction exerted by Pentecostalists on the poorest layers of the population. But his excessively optimistic hypothesis that Pentecostalism 'carries as much long term potential for becoming a religion or revolution as does liberationist Catholicism' (*Looking for God in Brazil. The Progressive Catholic Church in Urban Brazil's Religious Arena*, Berkeley: University of California Press, 1993, p. 226) is not shared by most recent analysts of this religious movement, who emphasize rather its conservative, authoritarian and manipulative character. See for instance André Corten, *Le Pentecôtisme au Brésil. Emotion du pauvre et romantisme théologique*, Paris: Karthala, 1995, and Jean-Pierre Bastian, *Le Protestantisme en Amérique Latine. Une approche socio-historique*, Geneva: Labor et Fides, 1994.

Conclusion: Is Liberation Theology Finished?

1 Daniel Levine, 'On Premature Reports of the Death of Liberation Theology', *The Review Of Politics*, vol. 57, no. 1, winter 1995, pp. 105–6.

2 In a recent contribution to this debate, Enrique Dussel has published an important book on the theological significance of Marx's concept of fetichism: *Las metáforas teológicas de Marx*, Estella (Navarra): Editorial Verbo Divino, 1993.

3 Jean Bertrand Aristide (with Christophe Wargny), *Tout homme est un homme*, Paris: Seuil, 1992, p. 95.

4 Ibid., p. 127.

5 Ibid., p. 108.

6 *Teología bíblica de la liberación*, Mexico: Editorial Jus, 1975.

7 *Proceso* (Mexico), 10 January 1994, p. 24.

8 Maurice Lemoine, 'La Révolte très politique des indiens d'équateur', *Le Monde Diplomatique*, November 1994, pp. 18–19.

9 François Normand, 'La Troublante ascension de l'Opus Dei', *Le Monde diplomatique*, September 1995, p. 23.

10 *La Documentation catholique*, no. 1884, November 1984, pp. 1064–73.

11 Ibid., pp. 1076–78.

12 *Cultures et foi*, no. 130–31, Summer 1989, pp. 17–18.

13 CEHILA, 'Déclaration de Santo Domingo', in *1492–1992. 500 ans d'évangélisation*, Paris: Comité Épiscopal France-Amérique latine, March 1990, no. 1, pp. 52–4.

14 Gustavo Gutiérrez, 'Vers le 5ème centennaire', in *1492–1992*, pp. 59–61.

15 CNBB, 'Das diretrizes a Santo Domingo', in *Documentos da CNBB*, no. 48, São Paulo: Edições Paulinas, 1992, pp. 18–19.

16 A very insightful presentation of these debates can be found in Father José Oscar Beozzo's, *A Igreja do Brasil. De João XXIII a João Paulo II, de Medellín a Santo Domingo*, Petrópolis: Vozes, 1994, pp. 314–20.

17 Clodovis Boff, 'Um ajuste pastoral', in *Santo Domingo. Ensaios teológico-pastorais*, Petropólis: Vozes, 1993, pp. 9–54.

18 Gustavo Gutiérrez, 'Documento: um corte transversal', in *Santo Domingo. Ensaios teológico-pastorais*, pp. 55–68.

19 Pablo Richard, 'La Iglesia Católica después de Santo Domingo', *Pasos* no. 44, November–December 1992; 'Las comunidades eclesiales de base en América Latina (después de Santo Domingo)', *Pasos*, no. 47, May–June 1993.

Index

Also of interest from Verso

DRAWING THE LINE
Art and Cultural Identity in Contemporary
Latin America
Oriana Baddeley and Valerie Fraser

I, RIGOBERTA MENCHÚ
An Indian Woman in Guatemala
Edited by Elisabeth Burgos-Debray

NOVAS TRAVESSIAS
Contemporary Brazilian Photography
Edited by Maria-Luiza Carvalho

THE LONG WAR
Dictatorship and Revolution in El Salvador
James Dunkerley

THE PACIFICATION OF CENTRAL AMERICA
James Dunkerley

POLITICAL SUICIDE IN LATIN AMERICA
James Dunkerley

POWER IN THE ISTHMUS
A Political History of Modern Central America
James Dunkerley

PLOTTING WOMEN
Gender and Representation in Mexico
Jean Franco

THE GATHERING OF VOICES
The Twentieth-century Poetry of Latin
America
Mike Gonzalez and David Treece

THE MOTORCYCLE DIARIES
A Journey around South America
Ernesto Che Guevara

CUBA
The Revolution in Peril
Janette Habel

MAGICAL REELS
A History of Cinema in Latin America
John King

JOURNEYS THROUGH THE LABYRINTH
Latin American Fiction in the Twentieth
Century
Gerald Martin

PASSION OF THE PEOPLE?
Football in South America
Tony Mason

JORGE LUIS BORGES
A Writer on the Edge
Beatriz Sarlo

MEMORY AND MODERNITY
Popular Culture in Latin America
William Rowe and Vivian Schelling

MISPLACED IDEAS
Essays in Brazilian Culture
Roberto Schwarz

DESIRE UNLIMITED
The Cinema of Pedro Almodóvar
Paul Julian Smith

VISION MACHINES
Cinema, Literature and Sexuality in Spain and
Cuba, 1983–1993
Paul Julian Smith

Printed in the United States
by Baker & Taylor Publisher Services